Scapegoat
The Persecuted Jew

A study of anti-Jewish prejudice—its history, causes, and remedies—written to people of faith by a Spirit-filled Christian of Jewish descent.

WhiteStone Publishing
Stonewood, WV, USA

Scapegoat
The Persecuted Jew

by Wesley G. Shaw, Ph.D.

ISBN-10: 1628830026

ISBN-13: 978-1628830026

Library of Congress Control Number: 2013946456

© 2013 WhiteStone Publishing
Stonewood, WV 26301-4831

All Scripture quotations in this book are from the
King James Version of the Bible unless otherwise identified.

All rights reserved. No portion of this publication may be reproduced,
stored in an electronic system or transmitted in any form or by any means,
electronic, mechanical, photocopy, recording, or otherwise, without the
prior permission of WhiteStone Publishing. Brief quotations may be
used in literary reviews.

This book may be purchased online. For a list of fine retailers, visit:
http://whitestonepublishing.com

Printed in United States of America.

Bookstores, online retailers, churches, etc., may purchase this book at
wholesale for resale purposes. For details & contact information, visit:
http://whitestonepublishing.com

CHRISTIAN RESOURCES | INSPIRATIONAL NOVELS | CHILDREN'S BOOKS

Table of Contents

Preface i
Introduction iii
1: History of Anti-Semitism 1
2: Jewish Isolation 19
3: Jewish "Superability" and "Arrogance" 31
4: Jewish Self-Hatred 41
5: Alleged Jewish Power and Nazi Anti-Semitism 47
6: Inadequate Views of the Holocaust 65
7: Remembering the Holocaust 73
8: Anti-Semitism in America Today 79
9: Combatting Anti-Semitism 85
10: Jesus Was a Jew 95
11: Judaism Today 99
12: Monotheistic Christianity as Judaism's Heir 111
13: The New Anti-Semitism 119
14: My Experience 129
    Dedication & Thanks 135
    Bibliography 137

Preface

Kike, Hebe, Sheeny—these are names shrouded in hate, envy, and ignorance. Although their use is indefensible, they fill a void in the lives of fearful souls who need a scapegoat. The hostility and prejudice toward Jews that they represent is a disease, the disease of anti-Semitism. Nothing new, it has existed for over two thousand years. Its climactic fervor in Nazi Germany culminated in the Holocaust, a murderous attempt to exterminate the Jewish people. Despite the defeat of the Nazis, the disease continues on, and without constant vigilance it has the propensity to spread to epidemic proportions even in our beloved America.

The purpose of this book is to examine anti-Semitism objectively in the light of the Scriptures to determine how these feelings of hate, envy, and alienation develop and produce such demonic results. At the same time we will endeavor to find some common ground where greater understanding and love may prevail.

Having been raised in an environment somewhat tainted by anti-Semitism, I have been exposed to all of the arguments expounded in its defense. In fact, I accepted them as true and rational until as a young adult I was informed that I was, in fact, part Jewish. It has been over twenty years since I learned this fact. In those twenty years, I have had much time to reflect on the disease. This book is the result of much soul searching. It is also a catharsis.

I have concluded that there is no rational justification for the arguments in favor of anti-Semitism. The simple repetition of untruths can make them seem valid, however. My purpose, therefore, is to bring each of these untruths to light and to expose their fallacy. At the same time I have attempted to uncover the factors that provide fertile ground for the germination of anti-Semitism in order that they may be abated.

Introduction

Less than seventy years ago, the world was shocked to learn that a modern, "civilized" state had orchestrated the murder of six million Jewish men, women, and children in a calculated effort to wipe out the entire race. The scope of this genocide becomes apparent when we realize that only about ten million Jews lived in the territories occupied by the Nazi perpetrators of this crime and that little more than three million Jews live in Israel today.

The Nazis treated Jews as worse than animals—terrorizing them, plundering and destroying their possessions, penning them up in concentration and extermination camps, torturing them cruelly, performing gruesome medical experiments on them, using them as slave labor, wantonly executing them en masse without regard to age or gender, using their skins for decorative purposes, mining the mouths of their corpses for gold, and committing many other atrocities.[1]

As horrifying and as incredible as this Holocaust is, it is only one dramatic, modern episode in a long history of persecution of the Jews. And the hostility toward Jews, or anti-Semitism, that prompted it still exists in our world today.

Introduction

The story of Anti-Semitism is a chronicle of pain, yet courageously confronting the buried demons that have made the Jews the scapegoat can lead Gentiles and Jews to greater mutual understanding and responsibility.

Even highly educated Gentiles are often unaware of the history of anti-Semitism, however, this is for the simple reason that they have never been taught. For example, in some histories of the Middle Ages and the crusades, the word *Jew* does not even appear. Catholic dictionaries and encyclopedias do not even list the term *anti-Semitism*.

The distinguishing mark of anti-Semitism, however concealed, is hatred. The term was given to the world in the bloody literature of Wilhelm Marr's *Victory of Judaism over Germanism*, published in Germany in 1879. Anti-Semites not only harbor racial antipathy toward Jews, but beginning some 2,300 years ago in the Hellenic world, they have labeled the Jews as physically, morally, and culturally inferior as well as unassimilable and corruptive by demagogues.

Is the Jew too persecution-minded? Was Hitler a latter-day aberration without roots in the past or connection with the present? To answer these and other questions, let us trace the development of anti-Semitism, which has indeed reached down to our own times.

NOTE

[1] William L. Shirer, *The Rise and Fall of the Third Reich* (New York: Simon and Shuster, 1960), pp. 937-94.

Chapter 1:
History of Anti-Semitism

"He...is persecuted, and none hindereth" (Isaiah 14:6).

The oppression and persecution of the Jews because of anti-Semitism is found in the Book of Esther. Haman, grand vizier under King Ahasuerus of Persia (486-465 B.C.) sought to kill all the Jews. This episode succinctly illustrates the classical reaction to the Jewish refusal to commingle with other cultures and to worship national gods. After the conquests of Alexander the Great (356-323 B.C.), in a world becoming Hellenized (Greek), the Jewish communities maintained their singularity of culture and continued to send personal taxes to Jerusalem, in their holy city.

Anti-Jewish sentiment appeared in third-century Egypt, the most advanced area of Hellenization outside of Greece. It was to Alexandria, Egypt, that 100,000 Jews were deported due to unsettled conditions in Palestine after Alexander's death, and there they soon became scapegoats. Although the Egyptians had a senate and governor of their own and grew wealthy with a monopoly in grain and navigation of the Nile, they, as well as the Greeks and Syrians, envied Jewish business success and resented their religious and social standards.[1]

Accusing Jews of being Egyptian lepers and diseased people was a dominant theme in the literature of pre-Christian anti-Semitism led by Apion and Tacitus. In the second century B.C., Mnaseas of Patros is said to have originated the fable that Jews adored the golden head of a donkey, while Agatharchides of Cnidus mockingly stated that Jerusalem was taken in 320 B.C. by Ptolemy Lagus because he attacked on the Sabbath and the Jews would not resist on that day—charges that have had a long future.[2]

The conflict between Hellas and Judea continued to grow, and in 175-163 B.C., there appeared a Hitler-like creature—the Seleucid ruler Antiochus IV Epiphanes, an extravagant Hellenizer—to pillage and slaughter in Jerusalem. He dedicated the Jewish temple to Jupiter Olympus and outlawed the practice of the Mosaic Law under the threat of death. The result was a violent Jewish reaction that ended in the astounding Maccabean victory, the first Jewish victory since 586 B.C. As a result the Jews enjoyed almost complete independence for about 75 years.

However, Hellenizing anti-Semites launched a literary wave of counterattack as the last pre-Christian century approached. Insidious and inhuman anti-Semitic epithets that reach down to the present day appeared in hate-filled literature. Apollonius Molon was the first to compose an entire work against the Jews. Polyhistor, Apion, Lysimachus, Chaeremon, Suidas, and Democritus added their terror and bitterness, and among many other accusations, the false charge of Jewish ritual murder was born.[3]

The Romans inherited Greek anti-Semitism with its revulsion against the Jewish insistence on leading a separate life, but their treatment of the Jews was more complex. The Jewish community in Rome before the Christian era was large and influential and voted in the assemblies. Their cohesiveness and business ability created wealth, converts, and imperial privileges. Jews were given the unique privilege to practice their monotheism and were released from secular activities on the Sabbath. Judaism was recognized as the only other religion in the empire except for the imperial cult itself. Even so, the Roman Empire was ambivalent toward Judaism, for the Romans were proud of their deities, their rites, and their own religion, which was strongly related to their daily lives. The cruel, anti-Semitic crucifixion of 2,000 Jews by Varus (A.D. 139-69) contrasted to concessions granted by Julius Caesar (100-44 B.C.) and Augustus (27 B.C.- A.D. 14) and considered to be the Jewish Magna Carta. Tiberius (A.D. 14-37) deported 4,000 Jews for malfeasance, and Caligula (A.D. 37-41) attempted to enforce emperor worship in the synagogues.

This religious tension exploded in the Judeo-Roman War, which ended with the destruction of Jerusalem by Vespasian and Titus in A.D. 70. One fortress, Masada, defied Rome for three years longer, but thousands of those who survived the war were transported to fight wild beasts in the amphitheaters or to slave to death in the Sinai mines.

To commemorate the conquest of Judea, the Torah was deposited in the palace of the emperor and Roman coins were inscribed "Judaea capta."[4] Hadrian followed in A.D. 117 with edicts to rebuild Jerusalem as a center of Roman culture and to ban the practice of circumcision, which led once again to rebellion and to the loss of half a million Jewish lives.

At the birth of Christianity, Jewish communities extended from Italy and Carthage in the west to Mesopotamia in the east and from the Black Sea in the north to Ethiopia in the south. About four million Jews lived in the Roman Empire; Palestine itself had a population of about three million. Christians saw the destruction of the temple as the fulfillment of Jesus Christ's prophecy and a confirmation of their belief that the scepter had passed from Israel to the church. In the second and third centuries, Christendom as a whole began to drift from its Jewish roots and the teachings of Scripture, and some professing Christians began to weave anti-Semitism into their theology.

After his "conversion" in 313, Emperor Constantine accelerated the paganization of Christian doctrine and lifestyle. He decided to establish a new capital in the east— Constantinople—which ultimately led to the founding of the Byzantine Empire. There the Jews were insulted and degraded, suffering some of their greatest agonies and being persecuted as a sacrilegious sect.[5] The Justinian Code eliminated the legal existence of Judaism and stripped it of its culture.

From the sixth century on, the Jews were thrown from place to place, uprooted, and left to search for a home. Both exile, or compulsory banishment, and diaspora, or voluntary scattering, have been part of Jewish existence from the earliest history of anti-Semitism.

An alien and disenfranchised people, debilitated by frequent persecutions and forced to abandon agriculture, their dispersion fitted them for trade. Their prominence and success in this field made them a target for abuse, however.

In seventh-century Arabia, Mohammed sought to propagate the new religion of Islam among the Jewish trading caravans. The Moslems gave Jews the alternatives of conversion or death. By 632, the year of Mohammed's death at the age of 61, Islam had subjugated Persia, much of the Byzantine world, part of Western Asia, and North Africa; then in 711 it crossed into Spain.[6]

Jews had prospered in Spain for centuries living in toleration and even respect before the conversion of the Visigoths to Roman Catholicism in 589. Itinerant Jewish traders had spread knowledge among the isolated barbarian tribes in various areas of Europe after the decline and fall of the Roman Empire, and by this time the Jews in Spain were well established, wealthy, and often holders of civil and military offices. The converted Visigoths established strong church-state ties and began a uniquely political policy of restrictions on Jews that later developed into full-blown persecution toward the end of the seventh century. Property was confiscated, discriminatory taxation imposed, and competition restricted.[7] The freedom of the Spanish Jews was restored, ironically, by the invasion of the Mohammedans in the eighth century, which led to a golden age of culture and wealth as Jews transmitted high-level administrative skills, scholarship, and goods between the Moslem and Christian worlds.[8]

Considered the most civilized country in Europe, Spain was invaded by Berber tribesmen who succeeded in destroying the capital and in forcing Jews, who were bitterly resented by the poor and uneducated, to seek refuge. After a century of glory, dynastic wars ensued, and when Toledo was captured in 1085, fanatical Berber tribes declared holy war on Jews.

The Jewish experience in Moslem Spain with years of tolerance and understanding disrupted by traumatic invasion and anti-Semitic repression has been marked by both the finest and most tragic aspects of Diaspora history in the medieval period. It is symbolic that Spanish-born Moses Maimonides (1135-1204), the greatest Jewish thinker of the Middle Ages, had to flee from persecution to Cairo and consequently graces the history of Egypt instead of Moorish Spain.[9]

Historians of the Jewish Middle Ages find themselves caught up in a reign of terror, confronted by man's inhumanity to man, as they approach the age of the crusades. "Most Christians have torn out of their history books the pages that Jews have memorized," pointed out Catholic priest Edward Flannery in the preface to the age of the crusades in his *History of the Jews*. For many Gentile scholars, the crusades present an expression of Christian courage, faith, and devotion to the redemption of the Holy Land. To the Jewish historian, this age presents the horror of fanatical crusaders running amok in pillaging, murdering, and forcibly converting Jews; of ecclesiastical legislation requiring Jews to wear distinctive, humiliating insignia and making them the target of any anti-Semitic mob; and of the onset of the rigorous enforcement of ghetto isolation. Historians simultaneously refer to this time as the Christian high Middle Ages and the Jewish dark ages, beginning with the crusades in the eleventh century and ending at the close of the fifteenth century. By the end of that period, Jews had been effectively excluded from the whole of Western Europe except parts of Germany and Italy.[10]

The motives behind the crusades were religious zeal, the desire of the Roman church to revitalize spiritual faith and subdue the Byzantine church, and the economic need to overthrow the Seljuks and Fatimids who blocked eastward trade monopolized by Constantinople. Pope Urban promised remission of sins to all participants, but lacking organization, the first crusade was a lawless mob. On the road eastward, it inaugurated a wholesale pogrom (massacre) against the Jews of the Rhineland. "Kill a Jew and save your soul," was the cry.[11] Even baptized Jews could not escape. Property was looted, houses were burned, and townsmen's promises of protection were broken.

Better organized in 1097, the crusaders pillaged along the route originally taken by Alexander the Great, defeated a great army of Seljuks, and captured Jerusalem on July 15, 1099, with epic slaughter. At the Holy Sepulchre, the crusaders declared the establishment of a Latin kingdom in Jerusalem as the Jewish population was herded into synagogues and burned alive.

The second crusade in 1147 was declared by Emperor Conrad III of Germany and King Louis VII of France, but it was thwarted by the Moslem sultan Saladin, who recaptured Jerusalem. The stage was thus set for the third crusade, a war of the cross against the crescent. Under the leadership of Richard the Lion-Hearted, with the ideals of religious hatred and a moratorium on all debts owed to Jews, the third crusade ended in failure too. Although the Christians regained the Palestine seacoast, Jerusalem remained a Moslem possession.

The anti-Semitism of the crusades was responsible for the murder of tens of thousands of European Jews. In Spain it conceived the Inquisition which "under the slaughterhouse efficiency" of Pope Sixtus IV in 1478 caused sword-point baptisms. The result was the Marranos, Jews who professed Christianity to avoid persecution or death but who often observed Judaism secretly. Under the reign of Ferdinand and Isabella, fifteenth-century Spain saw, in addition to the age-old religious anti-Semitism, a newer form of racial anti-Semitism with an insistence of "purity" of blood.[12] Jews were expelled from Spain in 1492 by royal decree, and their confiscated wealth was used to finance the voyage of Columbus to America.

The Catholic Church held that the Jews were nonbelievers and allowed the segregation of Jews in most towns and cities.

> Though Jews were unbelievers, the Church taught, they ought to be preserved to the end of days for they were necessary to the Christian world as witnesses to the truth of Christianity.... The popular mind, however, did not make such fine distinctions. It did not follow the doctrine of the Church, which

> combined toleration with discrimination and segregation. The ordinary citizen took the line that the Jews were both treacherous and unbelievers, and hence undesirable.... The ordinary man [would infer] that the Jews were double-faced and should be removed.[13]

The Jews, who for the most part would not convert or change from their beliefs, had a theological reason for not doing so—the hoped-for return to Jerusalem.

One more reason existed to hate Jews: the crucifixion of Jesus.

> Here again, the popular mind cast off all distinctions and nuances implicit in the ecclesiastical tradition, and presented the Jews as the Christ-killers, exclusively responsible for the crucifixion.... In the medieval passion plays, the Jew alone is responsible for the crucifixion.[14]

This image of the Jew as Christ-killer has probably been more responsible than anything else in perpetuating anti-Semitism. The devout Christians of the Middle Ages easily found an imagined reason to hate the local Jews in the biblical story of Jesus' death.

> The passion plays also presented the Jewish contemporaries of Jesus in medieval garb.... Through such tricks the authors succeeded in identifying, in the minds of their audience, the contemporary Jews with what they considered the greatest crime in history.[15]

Thus, the Middle Ages succeeded in creating a scapegoat for the many problems of the times. The Jews were there, and many people were already suspicious of them. It was an easy step to blame the Jews for a bad harvest or a plague.

> This explains why certain popular accusations like that of the Jews' poisoning wells were accepted at face value. During the Black Death (1348-1349) pestilence, Central and Western Europe lost more than a third of their populations.... Jews in Germany and in parts of Southern France, Spain and Italy were almost totally eliminated as a result of massacres brought on by that accusation.[16]

The persecution of the Jews was by no means a problem solely related to Spain, Russia, Germany, or any other country.

> The *universality* of anti-Semitism is attested to by innumerable facts, the most dramatic being that Jews have been expelled from nearly every country in which they have resided. Jews were expelled from England in 1290, France in 1306 and 1394, Hungary between 1349 and 1360, Austria in 1421, numerous localities in Germany between the 14th and 16th centuries.... Between 1948 and 1967 nearly all of the Jews of Aden, Algeria, Egypt, Iraq, Syria and Yemen, though not officially expelled, fled these countries.[17]

It appears that from the conversion of Europe to so-called Christianity in the eighth and ninth centuries, the Jews were outcasts. It is a strange but undeniable fact of our history.

> The permanence (as well as depth) of anti-Semitism is attested to by the obsessive attention given to the "Jewish Question" by anti-Semites throughout history. At one time or another nearly every one of the world's greatest powers that has had a large Jewish population has regarded this group, which never constituted more than a small percentage of the population, as an enemy. To the Roman Empire in the first century, the Christian world for over 15 centuries, the Nazi Reich, and to the Arabs, Muslims and the Soviet Union today, the Jews have been or are regarded as an insufferable threat.[18]

To achieve an understanding of the history of anti-Semitism, surely one must read *A Jew Today* by Elie Wiesel, journalist-philosopher-survivor-poet. He refers to the essence of Jewish history as mystical rather than rational, as its people should have, from a rational point of view, long ago yielded to the pressures and the laws of the enemy and agreed to leave the stage gracefully, as other ancient civilizations have done. He feels that the will of the Jews to survive in a society embarrassed and annoyed by their presence is basically due to the essence of being Jewish: "never to give up—never to yield to despair."[19]

In recent centuries, Eastern Europe has been the site of much persecution of the Jews. Poland had been a refuge for European Jews since the chartered protection of Boleslav in 1264, and about 500,000 Jews thrived there economically and culturally by the seventeenth century. Their prosperity provoked deep resentment among the Polish peasant masses, as Jews were rent collectors for the nobility and tax collectors for the government. Popular hatred burst into uninterrupted massacres of Jews.[20] Even when Poland was incorporated into the Russian empire, the Jewish population was restricted to the Pale of Settlement: they were ordered to cut off their beards, dress like Russians, teach Russian in their schools, and indoctrinate their youth with military and Russian religious practices. They were subjugated and repressed until the middle of the nineteenth century.

Many of these anti-Semitic policies were rescinded by Czar Alexander II, but his assassination in 1881 led to the beginning of a new era of mass riots called pogroms, in which thousands of Jews were killed. One of the greatest exoduses in history followed: almost one-third of all the Jews in Eastern Europe fled. In the early nineteenth century, nearly a hundred thousand Jews per year began leaving Russia, stopping temporarily in other countries but chiefly en route to the United States.

Seeking religious tolerance, the massive immigration of oppressed Jews spread out across America, but nearly a million settled in New York City. They were almost destitute financially, but they were skilled as workers, particularly in the garment industry, and they had a tradition of entrepreneurship and a determination "never to yield to despair." As a result, their rise to prosperity was unparalleled.[21] In New York, for example, where they constituted about one-fourth of the population, Jews comprised fifty-five percent of the doctors, sixty-four percent of the dentists, and sixty-five percent of the lawyers. Similar statistics were reflected in other major cities throughout the United States. Jews created the motion-picture industry and many others.

At the same time, anti-Semitism began to increase in the U. S. against not only the Eastern European Jewish immigrants because of their foreign lifestyle, dress, and language, but against Jews in general. They were barred from occupations, businesses, and social settings, and they were never allowed to dominate the huge American economy.[22] Even so Israel, the historic Jewish homeland, has to a large degree been built by the financial and political support of the Jews in America.

Germany was historically considered one of the most tolerant European countries for "the wandering Jew," and yet there anti-Semitism reached its height of catastrophe in the twentieth-century Nazi Holocaust.[23]

In 1146, when the first crusades brought massive violence and expulsion to the Jews in Germany, some German nobles protected them in their castles. In the seventeenth and eighteenth centuries there were court Jews who served kings in various ways, but their careers or fortunes or lives could be ended by a whim.[24]

Germany was one of the most important centers of Jewry for centuries. In the Hebrew language, the word *Ashkenaz* means Germany, and therefore German Jews were called Ashkenazic Jews. Significantly, with the exception of the Sephardic Jews from Spain, most of the Jews of Europe and of the world are called Ashkenazic

Jews. The Yiddish language originated in Germany in the twelfth century, and it was from here that Reform Judaism and Zionism later evolved. By the end of the nineteenth century there were nearly 600, 000 Jews in Germany, "prosperous, German-speaking and German-feeling, with more than half of them in commerce, one-fifth in industry and trade, and about 6 percent in liberal professions and public service." Nearly half of all Jewish marriages in Germany were to Gentiles, thousands converted to Christianity, and there appeared to be widespread social acceptance.[25] (Does not this situation bear a striking similarity to conditions in America today?)

When the economic crisis and collapse of the Weimar Republic brought the ruthless, half-crazed Adolph Hitler to power, however, the German people embraced the Nazi Party. Its purpose was to smash the Republic, rebuild the military strength of Germany, defy the Allies, drive the Jews out of the country, and completely annihilate one of the most cultured and valuable Jewish settlements in the West. To a great extent it succeeded.

Nineteenth- and twentieth-century anti-Semitism came as a bitter blow to the Jews of Europe who had hoped that, as citizens, the society in which they lived would accept them, but centuries of hatred, discrimination, and persecution were exacerbated by economic crisis and political insecurity. The medieval myths that die hard led to the final extreme measure: physical annihilation in the German Holocaust. The most vigorous anti-Semitism stemmed from the theory of racism, used at its zenith in conservative German nationalism. This theory provided biological "proof" of the racial superiority of Germans and of the racial inferiority of Jews. The Aryan myth claimed that the Roman, Germanic, and Slavic people shared the pristine purity of the blond, blue-eyed Nordic, which was inherently superior to the short, black-haired, dark-eyed Jew, and also shared a common language source.[26] This prejudice against the Jews was aided by statements of two famous Germans of the past—Luther and Wagner.

The eminent composer Richard Wagner had a terrific impact on the German people. Although he certainly had help from Jews in getting his operas performed, he became the forerunner and high priest of the Nordic racialist cult and imbued Hitler's intense nationalism. In his polemical essay "Judaism in Music," he pointed out what he considered Jewish dangers and warned Germans against racial degeneration. "We may explain the decay of the German folk by the fact that it is now exposed without defense to the penetration of the Jew."[27] His theory perpetuated the fear that German blood was in danger of contamination by physical contact with Jews and that intermarriage would result in the subversive decay of the German nation.

Martin Luther, the vigorous Protestant reformer, had at first been sympathetic toward the Jews. Drawing from the medieval era, the Protestant Reformation depended on Jewish scholarship to guide its understanding of the Bible in the original Hebrew, and efforts were made to convert the Jews of Germany. Public opinion stirred the church on the whole question of freedom of thought. Luther denounced the Catholic clergy for their brutal and senseless rantings against the Jews:

> The Jews are the best blood on earth; through them alone the Holy Ghost wished to give all the books of Holy Scripture to the world; they are the children, and we are the guests and the strangers.[28]

In his renowned pamphlet *Jesus was Born a Jew*, which has been republished many times, Luther gave hope to the Jewish people:

> If we would help them, so must we exercise, not the law of the Pope, but that of Christian love—show them a friendly spirit, permit them to live and to work, so that they have cause and means to be with us and amongst us.... And if some remain obstinate, what of it? Not every one of us is a good Christian.[29]

Luther's desire was to convert the Jews, but they proved no more agreeable to persuasion than to force. Like Mohammed, he had expected to convert them, but disappointed in his expectations, he too turned on them with a savage fury: "What shall we Christians do with this damned, rejected race?" In the most vituperative language, he demanded that the German state burn their synagogues, homes, and books, forbid their rabbis to teach, refuse to let them travel, compel them to renounce banking and finance, and force them to be expelled as France, Spain, and Bohemia had done.[30]

Luther forced the passage of an entire battery of legislation that required Jews to live in ghettos, wear discriminatory yellow badges, pay heavier taxes than Christians, and place identifying signs of a donkey or garlic on their homes. His tyranny became part of the inheritance he left to his followers, and his anti-Semitic writings played into the hands of the Nazis.

Later Protestant leaders, many of whom broke with Luther over doctrinal issues, did not adopt or express his views concerning Jews. Nevertheless, it is historically true that professing Christians of Catholic, Orthodox, and Protestant affiliation have often promoted anti-Semitism. Of course, anti-Semitism is incompatible with true Christianity as expressed in the New Testament and as practiced by apostolic, biblical Christians today.

In the next few chapters we will discuss important factors that have contributed to and accompanied anti-Semitism. Our study will show that none of these factors can justify anti-Jewish attitudes or behavior.

NOTES

[1] Edward H. Flannery, *The Anguish of the Jews* (New York: Macmillan, 1965), pp. 3-7.
[2] Ibid., p. 8.
[3] Ibid., p. 12.
[4] Abram L. Sachar, *A History of the Jews* (New York: Alfred A. Knoff, 1974), pp. 112-123.

[5] Abba Eban, *The Story of the Jews* (New York: Behrman House, 1968), p. 123.
[6] Solomon Grayzel, *A History of the Jews* (New York: Mentor Books, 1968), pp. 270-71.
[7] Ibid., p. 212.
[8] Ibid., pp. 290-92.
[9] Frederick M. Schweitzer, *A History of the Jews* (New York: Macmillan, 1971), p. 63.
[10] Eban, p. 187.
[11] Ibid., p. 176.
[12] Frederick M. Schweitzer, p. 106.
[13] Salo W. Baron, "Medieval Folklore and Jewish Fate," in *Jewish Heritage Reader*, ed. by Lily Edelman (New York: Taplinger Publishing Co., 1965), p. 178.
[14] Ibid., pp. 178-79.
[15] Ibid., p. 179.
[16] Ibid., p. 180.
[17] Dennis Prager and Joseph Telushkin, *Why the Jews?* (New York: Simon and Schuster, 1983), p. 18.
[18] Ibid., p. 20.
[19] Elie Wiesel, *A Jew Today* (New York: Random House, 1978), p. 164.
[20] Thomas Sowell, *The Economics and Politics of Race* (New York: Quill Publishers, 1983), p. 89.
[21] Ibid., pp. 90-91.
[22] Max Dimont, *The Jews in America* (New York: Simon and Schuster, 1978), pp. 223-26.
[23] Sowell, pp. 84-86.
[24] Ibid., p. 87.
[25] Ibid.
[26] Eban, p. 287.
[27] Quoted in Schweitzer, p. 213.
[28] Quoted in Sacher, p. 228.
[29] Ibid.
[30] Schweitzer, p. 129.

Chapter 2:
Jewish Isolation

The isolation, cultural differences, and material and cultural success of Jews have contributed to anti-Semitism.

Jewish isolation is epitomized by the ghetto, the section in many European cities to which Jews were formerly restricted. The term *ghetto* appears to have originated from the Italian word *geto*, meaning "iron foundry," as the first ghetto in Venice was located beside one.[1]

However, Jewish isolation was originally a voluntary reality dating back to the Hellenic era of Alexander the Great (356-323 B.C.). Unlike the rest of their Greco-Oriental and later Roman neighbors, Jews did not take their place as average citizens of towns and cities but chose to acknowledge Jerusalem as the holy city, sending personal taxes to the temple, where their one true God would receive undying respect and devotion. The Jews looked upon their host countries as profane soil and their fellow citizens as superstitious and ignorant. Jews grouped themselves in a certain quarter of the cities, but the Greeks perceived this aloofness as arrogance. The Greeks resented rival claims to superiority or privilege by people that they considered politically and culturally undistinguished, who refused to accept common religious and social standards.

In the ancient world, the Hellenic city Alexandria became the chief center of anti-Semitism. The litanies of pre-Christian anti-Semitism tried to establish a humiliating origin for the Jews, asserting that Moses taught "these Egyptian lepers" not to adore the gods, to abstain from sacred animals, and to have nothing to do with those not of their faith.

In the Middle Ages, Jewish life was formally regulated by the Third (1179) and Fourth (1215) Lateran Councils of the Roman Catholic Church, which constituted the high-water mark of anti-Jewish legislation in that period.[2] Christian households could not employ Jewish maids, nurses, or physicians, and Jews had to live apart from Christians. Usury was condemned. In the 1215 legislation, Jews were forbidden to appear in public on certain holy days of the church calendar, nor could Jews hold public office or have any authority over Christians. The measure was intended to end the "court" or "privileged" status of Jews in the service of many kings and feudal lords. Above all, the Jew legally had to wear distinctive dress, which included a large, peaked, crimson hat. A yellow or crimson circle had to be attached to his clothing as a symbol of the Dantesque circle of hell to which he was presumably condemned. This pariah status of the Jew made him the obvious target for any mob.

Chapter 2 - Jewish Isolation

In this environment, the ghetto, often referred to as "the inferno" by historians, became a strategy for Jewish existence and survival.³ During the crusades, Jews petitioned for separate quarters within the towns as their own, which, they felt, would afford them safeguards against any diminution in the ranks of the faithful. Jews of Rome were first forced to live in a section near the Tiber on July 26, 1552.

The ghetto created a close-knit Jewish community, although its primary purpose was to separate Christians from Jews. It was walled, and its gates were guarded by Christian gatekeepers who locked the inhabitants in at night and during Christian festivals. During the day, Jews could leave to conduct their business outside, and Gentiles came in.

The main effects of this separation were deleterious culturally. Within narrow confines, Jewish life became introverted. As Jews were cut off from fully participating in the larger world, they concentrated their life on the past. Although the ghetto fostered ethnic solidarity, an attachment to the synagogue, and a devotion to study, which in time became the very basis for survival, the ghetto mentality was the inevitable result, as well as another basis for anti-Semitism. Most inmates looked upon Gentile outsiders with deep suspicion, hatred, and envy.⁴

There was a high degree of inbreeding—physical, social, and intellectual. By the time the ghetto had been in existence for a couple of centuries, it was possible to see the results physically: the typical Jew had declined. He had lost inches off his stature; he had acquired a perpetual stoop; he had become timorous and, in many cases, neurotic.

Degrading occupations originally imposed by law, such as dealing in old clothes and moneylending, became the Jew's only recourse for survival. His sense of solidarity with his fellow Jews became fantastically exaggerated and was accompanied in most cases by a perpetual sense of grievance against the Gentile, who was responsible for his lot.[5] Hermetically sealed off from their hostile environment, Jewish merchants and financiers were resented as competitors, rather than monopolists, and most trades and professions remained closed to them. Moreover, by the sixteenth century, Judaism had become more and more a closed system of thought.

Expulsions from Spain and Portugal led the Jewish dispersion toward the Balkans, Poland, Turkey, and Palestine, as anti-Semitism remained endemic in France and England. However, Jews held a certain affinity with English Puritans, who laid a heavy accent on the Old Testament in their worship. Cromwell, who considered the benefits that Jews might bring to the economy of his country, permitted the Marranos (converts to Christianity under duress) to establish a synagogue and increase. His action aroused great public debate, as traditional accusations were revived and Jews were accused of buying up cathedrals after having been admitted, it appeared, by the back door. Nevertheless, the foundation of the English Jewish community was laid.

With the invention of the printing press, Jewish and Christian scholars met on an academic level. In Germany, Johann Reuchlin, one of the most highly regarded humanists of the time, became embroiled in a fierce defense of the Talmud against traditional prejudice. The most noted humanist, Erasmus of Rotterdam, described the prevailing prejudice: "If it is Christian to hate the Jews, then we are all good Christians."[6] The Talmud was a chief focus of anti-Semitism because it took Judaism out of the Gentile mainstream of history and culture and prevented Jewish participation in the common intellectual life.

After the Thirty Years' War, when numerous petty princes in Germany competed for power and wealth, every prince and many cardinals and bishops had court Jews who were financiers and who administered the economic affairs of the court. These Jews acquired great prestige and wealth. Wolf Werthheimer, a Munich banker, was one of the most famous and was able to intercede in expulsion orders issued in 1747.

The majority of Jews remained in ghettos where new civil restrictions were added to their rigidly regulated life: Jews could not appear in public when a prince was in town, could not buy ahead of a Christian at the market, could not walk in twos, had to have a safe-conduct pass, had to pay a body tax in transit, and had to wear prescribed clothing. More drastic were laws that regulated their marriage, designed to prevent too rapid multiplication of Jews. In some cases, Jewish marriages were limited to the number of deaths and, in others, only the oldest son was allowed to marry. Even the number of wedding guests was limited. Only one or two sons were allowed to inherit. Johann Eisinminger's *Judaism Unmasked*, published in this era, was a veritable treasure trove for anti-Semites.[7]

Pope Paul IV manifested great zeal against the Jews, and few popes compare with him for severity toward them. Not only did he sustain the campaign against the Talmud, but he forbade Jews to own land or to converse with Christians. Conditions for Italian Jews could not be distinguished from the downtrodden state of Jewry in other European countries.

In this age of wandering there was also a brutal attempt to extinguish the Jews of Poland. By the late Middle Ages, the light of hope for a peaceful existence was fading again.

Jews in Poland formed a middle class of traders and financiers between the nobles and peasants and had been appointed official agents and tax collectors, but the church, alarmed by their ascendancy, imposed canonical restrictions.[8] However, in the sixteenth century, Jews were still too well integrated into the socioeconomic complex of the nation to be dispensed with. Jewish education reached such a degree of excellence that they became envied, and charges of ritual murder and host desecration became the basis of uprisings. From 1648 to 1658 came one of the bloodiest decades in anti-Semitic history, as Jews were caught in a crossfire between the Eastern Orthodox Cossacks of the Ukraine and the Polish Catholics. The Jews were ravaged in Poland, and the death toll reached a staggering 500,000, as refugees swarmed toward the west and north.[9]

The partition of Poland, made possible by economic weakness and internal chaos, was accomplished by Austria, Prussia, and Russia by 1795. Even in the last struggle, Jews fought shoulder to shoulder under Kosciuszko with their former persecutors, and a Jewish legion of 500 light cavalry under Berek Joselovitz was outstanding in defense of the doomed Polish capital. Nearly a million Polish Jews came under the control of Catherine II of Russia, despite her *kromye zydov* legislation (literally "without Jews") by which she attempted to confine them to a limited district and forbade them to join merchant and artisan guilds.

Russian peasants complained that Jews were enslaving them, and nobles used Jews as scapegoats to evade complaints against their own harshness. Derzhavin declared in his *Opinion* that the Jews were a menace to Russian progress because they were middlemen and economic parasites and that because they were trained exclusively in the Bible and Talmud, they were clannish and unassimilable. He proposed to restrict Jewish occupations and uproot the Talmudic educational system.[10]

After the accession of Alexander I in 1801, Jews could buy unoccupied land and take part in schools where the language of instruction was Russian, Polish, or German. When Napoleon's army from France invaded Russia, the Jews loyally supported the government, but after Waterloo, Alexander became alarmed by a reactionary movement in which thousands of southern Russians turned to practices resembling Judaism. As a result, 20,000 Jewish families of Moghilev and Vitebsk were expelled to the Jewish pale. A small number of wealthier Jews carried on trade in furs and skins, but the Jewish masses were hemmed into a narrow district and repressed by anti-Semitism.

Nicholas I despised Jews as economic leeches and as an unassimilable element and began a relentless thirty years' war against them. By compulsory conscription into the Russian army, they were transported long distances from their native towns and away from every Jewish influence. They were beaten, served salt foods, and denied water; thousands were forced to convert. Adding to their demoralization, Russian law provided that the recruiting war be done for the *kahal*, or government centers, by *lovchiki*, or catchers. The lovchiki were Jews who preyed on fellow Jews in a new form of terrorist anti-Semitism.[11] When Nicholas' attempt to establish secular schools to eradicate the traditional system of Jewish education failed, his laws of 1851 led to the expulsion of 150,000 Jews who were not in "productive" occupations. Literary anti-Semitism fueled prejudice.

With the accession of Alexander II, conscription was made equal for both Christians and Jews, Jews were allowed to enter the professions of law and medicine, and Jewish periodicals could be published in the Russian language. However, this liberalism encouraged anti-Semitic dissension and did not break down Jewish solidarity. There was an outcry against Jewish financiers for exploiting mines, building railroads, and investing in their own economic advance. Accusations of ritual murder appeared again.

Under Alexander III, Pobedonostsev, his anti-Semitic chief advisor, turned Russia to the depths of absolutism, making all Jewry the target: one third was to emigrate, one third to die, and one third to be converted. Blaming Jewish exploitation of the peasants as the cause, the first pogrom struck masses of Jews in the name of the Orthodox Church on Easter of 1881. Ignatiev, minister of the interior, claimed this was the natural consequence of the unfair economic practices of the Jews. He issued the "Temporary Rules" in May 1882, which decreed that Jews could not settle outside of towns but must be interned in their village ghettos, that they could not own mortgages or leases, that any claims they already had were cancelled without compensation, and that they could not attend universities except for a limited quota of three percent. The pogroms, as a solution to the Jewish "problem," continued to 1891.[12]

During this period, about 100,000 Jews immigrated to the United States, as Russian leaders wanted their cities "judenrein," cleansed of Jews. Barom Moritz de Hirsch, one of Europe's wealthiest Jews, attempted to spend millions on a plan with the London Colonization Society in 1891 to remove the majority of Russian Jews to Argentina at the rate of about 25,000 annually. Thus a civilized government sought to remove a whole population.

Nicholas II inaugurated the two bloodiest decades of the Jews in Russia. By the end of the century, Jewish economic life had been demoralized to a point that in a race always too proud to beg, the census of 1897 revealed that 37.7 percent required Passover aid.[13] The League of the Russian People, known as the "Black Hundreds," was organized in 1904 to combat both constitutionalism and the Jews, and it perpetuated assassinations and pogroms. Mendel Beilis's trial and acquittal for ritual murder in 1911 brought Russia's foremost writers to speak out against anti-Semitism.

The so-called *Protocols of the Learned Elders of Zion* is one of the chief source books for twentieth-century anti-Semitism. Printed by the Russian government in 1905, it consists of a series of 24 lectures on alleged Jewish plans for subjugating the world and establishing a Jewish world state. It includes supposed examples and methods for stupefying Gentiles and controlling the press, finance, and government. Its original purpose was to influence the Czar against the allegedly "Jewish-Masonic" constitutional government, and by 1919 it was translated into German, French, Polish, Italian, Japanese, and Arabic to discredit Jews throughout Europe. It was given the widest circulation in the United States by Henry Ford in his Dearborn Independent. Although proven to be "the greatest forgery of the century" by the London Times in 1921, it later reached the peak of its influence in Nazi Germany.[14]

This question of international conspiracy or control by Jews originated in history when Jews first began to emerge from the ghettos of Europe during the industrial revolution. Equipped by their past struggles, many Jews entered the rugged competition of commercial and financial enterprises, and most countries had a powerful Jewish financier. The House of Rothschild spread its operations throughout Europe. There were charges of a worldwide Jewish financial conspiracy as the expanding economy began to foster Jewish liberation. Historian Abram Sachar explained, "Economic changes were more crucial in winning political equality for Jews than all the glittering generality about the rights of man and the sanity of the human personality."[15] The charge that Jews had control of the international traffic in gold in order to wield power over the Christians was made in view of the success of the Montefiores, Goldsmids, and Solomons in England, the Pereires in France, and the Bischoffsheims in Germany. Even the influence of Benjamin Disraeli, who had risen from humble beginnings to become the English prime minister and was a converted Jew, did not stem the flow of anti-Semitism.

In summary, the cultural distinctiveness of the Jews originated in their desire to maintain a biblical way of life and worship the one true God in a polytheistic, Hellenistic world and later in a professing Christian world that had largely departed from the doctrine and ethics of Jesus. This cultural uniqueness has unjustifiably been a factor in anti-Semitism, as Gentiles have often viewed Jewish distinctives with suspicion and sometimes envy. Extreme physical and cultural isolation of Jews in Europe was largely the result of anti-Semitism, however, and so is particularly inappropriate to use as a rationale for anti-Semitism. Moreover, many other ethnic groups today have a similar desire to preserve their identity and are rightly encouraged to do so.

Jewish material success can be largely attributed to values Jews have derived from the Scriptures as well as from adversity. Even their historical success in trade and finance stems in large part from medieval restrictions that forced them into these fields. Due to the possibility of confiscations, attacks, and expulsions, as well as later ghetto laws, owning farmland was generally impractical, and Jews were barred by law from many desirable occupations. Moreover, Jewish success has often been exaggerated, and myths of their power have been perpetuated by blatant lies and forgeries. Thus, as subsequent chapters will discuss further, Jewish success, ability, and power are not valid reasons for anti-Semitism either.

NOTES

[1] Edward H. Flannery, *The Anguish of the Jews* (New York: Macmillan, 1965), p. 6.
[2] Frederick Schweitzer, *A History of the Jews* (New York: Macmillan, 1971), p. 88.
[3] Lucy Dawidowicz, *The War Against the Jews*, 1933-1945 (New York: Holt, Rinehart, and Winston, 1975), p. 200.
[4] Cecil Roth, *A History of the Jewish People* (Oxford: East and West Publications, 1935), pp. 308.
[5] Ibid., p. 309.
[6] Hans J. Schoeps, *The Jewish-Christian Argument* (New York: Holt, Rinehart, and Winston, 1963), p. 24.
[7] Ibid., p. 25.
[8] Ibid., p. 29.
[9] Ibid., p. 30.
[10] Abram Sachar, *A History of the Jews* (New York: Alfred A. Knopf, 1974), p. 312.
[11] Ibid., p. 314.
[12] Ibid., p. 319.
[13] Ibid., p. 320.
[14] Raul Hilberg, *The Destruction of European Jews* (New York: Quadrangle Press, 1961), p. 59.
[15] Sachar, p. 100.

Chapter 3:
Jewish "Superability" and "Arrogance"

"A sound heart is the life of the flesh: but envy the rottenness of the bones" (Proverbs 14:30).

A factor that contributed to anti-Semitism in pre-war Europe and America is the belief that many Jewish people have superability and a degree of arrogance. Few myths are wholly the products of thin air; is it then reasonable to assume that in some ineffable and ironic fashion the Jews have wrought their own persecution through certain actions, values, and standards they have selected? Some evidence exists for this statement; the very success of the Jews in prewar Europe and in America certainly aroused envy and hatred in groups less able to compete, especially in difficult economic times that have plagued the industrial states in the modern era.

The "high quality" of Jewish life has often been the subject of comment. Different reasons have been offered as to causes for this phenomenon. This quality of life derives, it is held, from the ability of the Jews to attain success despite so many obstacles. One Jewish author said that the success of Jewish immigrants in the New World is "the greatest collective Horatio Alger story in American history."[1] Apparently, he did not merely mean that Jews have somehow enjoyed disproportionate success over other ethnic entities, but rather that their success can be attributed to the distinctive abilities and values held by Jews.[2]

Particular values are often attributed to Jewish families as well as to Jewish culture as a whole, culture being the traditional means of transmitting the developing children those norms and standards upon which ability and aptitudes are predicated. Sociologists have long pointed out the strength of the Jewish family. For example, the divorce rate among religious Jews is low in comparison to non-Jewish society. The stability and closeness of the Jewish family has been evident in prewar Europe, among immigrants to American shores, and to a considerable degree even in the present day.[3] Such an environment gives young children a firm basis on which to exercise their natural talents. It might also provoke hostility among those groups in which home life tends to be more disruptive and divisive.

The myth of Jewish superability has sprung from the values already noted. These values were firmly in place in Europe before World War II as well as among those Jews who settled in America. Thrift, sobriety, ambition, desire

Chapter 3 - Jewish "Superability" and "Arrogance"

for education, ability to postpone immediate gratification for the sake of long-range goals, and aversion to violence are among them. Rather than super abilities themselves, "it is these cultural values which account for the rapid rise of the Jews in occupational status and economic affluence."[4]

Unfortunately, neither European nor American racists distinguished this value orientation from inherent superiority and a subsequent belief that Jews by virtue of seemingly superior attributes were arrogant and overly proud of success.

If but one value can be equated with so-called "superability" on the part of the Jews, that commitment would be stress on education. Jews have valued education not so much as a pathway to success but instead as the route to a religious and moral lifestyle. The monetary rewards placed on high educational abilities by the modern world have come merely as an accompaniment to the main goal of education as a religious responsibility. In the ancient and medieval ages, when most of their neighbors were illiterate, the Jews, at great sacrifice in some cases, expended money and effort in the education of their sons and daughters. They prolonged schooling as much as possible. When education became a generalized institution and available to nearly everyone in the modern, developed states, the Jews, with their tradition of placing high value on schooling, were in a favorable position to take advantage of the rewards it afforded.[5]

It is not then surprising that Jews appear to be overly represented in certain desirable professional fields. American Jews have been twice as apt to attend college as their non-Jewish counterparts. As a result, while composing only three percent of the population in the United States, Jews are "overrepresented" in medicine by 231 percent in proportion to the general population; in psychiatry by 478 percent; in law by 265 percent. The high visibility of Jews in these and similar elite fields of endeavor have, both in the Europe of the 1920s and 1930s and in America, led to belief in a superior level of intelligence—and aroused a dangerous hostility in "out" groups of society.[6]

The numbers of Jews who seem to possess superability, as measured by their concentration in prestige careers, served to obscure the negative side of the Jewish success story; one side of the myth was not brought out, either by the Nazis in Germany or in the more discreetly veiled prejudice of the United States. In both countries, the bulk of the Jewish middle class was—and is—concentrated in small business; large numbers are employed in manual work or in low-paying, white-collar, clerical occupations. In prewar Europe and in the United States today, few Jews are found in the managerial hierarchies of major corporations. Many Jews live in poverty; in America the number is estimated at present to be some 800,000. Most of these are elderly and have never managed to escape poverty. In prewar Germany, even larger portions of the Jewish population were poor. Many of these were immigrants from Eastern Europe who lacked skills necessary for success in urban society. Thus, immersion in Jewish culture and values does not guarantee an escape from a low standard of living.[7]

A non-Jewish American who looks at the history of Jewish immigration between 1881 and 1924 has perhaps

Chapter 3 - Jewish "Superability" and "Arrogance"

some cause for ascribing superability to Jews as a group. When they first came, "the Jews were scarcely distinguishable from the huge mass of depressed arrivals," arriving without capital, without marketable skills, illiterate, and impoverished. And yet they achieved the American Dream far ahead of, and in greater proportion than, immigrants from other cultures. This apparent superior ability to forge ahead regardless of obstacles might well spring from the need of the Jews for over 2,000 years to adjust and to cope with living "as strangers among other peoples."[8]

The charge that Jews are arrogant or excessively proud of their success can be traced to several possible roots. As with other minority cultures, the Jews in prewar Europe and in the United States tended to cling to their heritage. In part, the idea of separatism was thrust upon them by mainstream society; Jews had long been forced to reside in ghettos set apart from dominant groups. Too, there was more safety for the Jews in this arrangement; it was more comfortable to live among those of like customs, habits, and language. Even when Jews became successful and had the means to find housing outside the ghetto, some did not wish to leave friends and relations behind. Conversely, many Christian neighborhoods sought ways to block Jewish "invasion" of particular areas, as by the so-called gentleman's agreements. The result even when not desired by the Jews themselves, was inevitable: people set apart are viewed as "different" by others. Since Jews did not mix with the mainstream, especially when they were restricted and not allowed to do so, they were denounced as proud and arrogant. This charge of arrogance seemed especially plausible since Jews had obvious possible sources of pride—high quality of family life, values, education, and material success—that aroused envy in others.[9]

Moreover, as a distinct culture always in the minority, the Jews of prewar Europe and in the United States existed under the threat of the destruction of their culture, perhaps not through pogroms and similar outpourings of hostility, but through attenuation. The weakening of a unique way of life can stem from a number of mechanisms. As people grow more open to outside influences that inevitably come through education and mass communication, traditional values and norms—their culture as a whole—come under fire. Religion and community consciousness decline, and intermarriage occurs with increasing frequency.

In the face of what they perceive as the danger of cultural breakdown, Jewish parents may strongly hope their children will not marry non-Jews. When dating begins, Jewish parents may encourage their children to mix socially only with members of their own group.

Sometimes non-Jewish teenagers interpret this tendency as exclusiveness, clannishness, or elitism. They feel hurt by what they perceive as personal rejection and may take on anti-Semitic attitudes in reaction. On the other hand, the concern of Jewish parents about the possibility of intermarriage and the subsequent loss of culture is well founded. About one-third of young Jews in the United States do marry outside their faith.[10] Such high rates of intermarriage do seem a threat to the future of the Jewish community to some degree. Thus, what is seen as Jewish arrogance actually stems from an understandable desire to protect the group as a whole from influences that place its continuation in jeopardy.

It is true that Jewish separateness, which has often resulted in the myth of "proud, upstart" Jews, was not always forced upon them by anti-Semitic governments and peoples. "It was frequently the chosen position of the chosen people." Their belief in their chosenness and their strict dietary laws served to cut Jews off from the larger environment. Although the most rigid of the prohibitions that governed Jewish transactions with Gentiles through the years and that could be observed when large groups of Jews lived in close proximity and were economically self-sufficient were eventually modified to accommodate to the larger society, contacts between the two communities tended to be for business only.[11] Because of stringent bars dating from at least the Middle Ages, social segregation between Jews and Gentiles was as total as their religious separateness. At least one writer believes that the "shunning of Gentiles," while perhaps saving the Jewish identity, "killed many Jews in the process." The aloofness of the Jews, together with the mysterious nature of their religion, made them an enigma to their non-Jewish neighbors. And it is a well-known truism that what is not known or understood might well become hated by those outside the perceived inner circle.[12]

Finally, even in the ashes of the Holocaust, many would see further "proof" of Jewish arrogance. It is charged that the Jews have made too much of their undenied suffering. Blacks, for example, point out that they too have endured the often unendurable. Poles note that more Polish Gentiles lost their lives in World War II than did

Polish Jews. Yet the Jews seem to see their pain as unique and special and refuse to let the rest of the world forget what it would prefer to relegate to dead history. This insistence is sometimes attributed to Jewish pride—a feeling that they have a lock on misery and, like a dog with a bone, will not relinquish their hold. Nevertheless, no other people have been persecuted for so long and with such murderous efficiency.

Several writers have asserted that Jewish "arrogance," the pride that did not allow them to assimilate, has led to their persecution. But assimilation would not have preserved the Jews of Nazi Germany and World War II Europe. Yet, citing the example of over 100,000 Jews who were "forcibly converted to Catholicism during the Spanish Inquisition in the fifteen century and disappeared as Jews," some argue that "throughout Jewish history Jews who assimilated escaped anti-Semitic persecution."[13]

It is twisted logic, however, to claim that the Jews are responsible for their own problems because of their refusal to bow to the non-Jewish majority's national and religious identity. It is not arrogance for a people to seek to preserve their cultural identity; to the contrary, those who demand universal and total conformity to the culture of the majority may well be guilty of the charge.

Chapter 3 - Jewish "Superability" and "Arrogance"

NOTES

[1] Milton M. Gordon, *Assimilation in American Life* (New York: Oxford University Press, 1964), p. 185.

[2] Ibid., pp. 186-87.

[3] Marshall Sklare, *America's Jews* (New York: Random House, 1971), pp. 94-96.

[4] Gordon, pp. 186-88.

[5] Thomas Sowell, Race and Economics (New York: David McKay, 1975), pp. 62-75.

[6] Dennis Prager and Joseph Telushkin, *Why the Jews?: The Reason for Antisemitism* (New York: Simon & Schuster, 1983), pp. 48-50.

[7] Naomi Levine and Martin Hochbaum, *Poor Jews* (New Brunswick, N.J.: Transaction Books, 1974), pp. 21-37.

[8] Sklare, *America's Jews,* pp. 59-61.

[9] Marshall Sklare, ed. *The Jews* (New York: Free Press, 1958), pp. 140-45.

[10] Sklare, *America's Jews,* pp. 182-9 1.

[11] Jacob Katz, *Exclusiveness and Tolerance: Jewish-Gentile Relations in Medieval and Modern Times* (New York: Schocken, 1962), pp. 40-43.

[12] Ibid., p. 43.

[13] Prager and Telushkin, pp. 180-81.

Chapter 4:
Jewish Self-Hatred

Hatred against the Jewish people has been so forceful over time that in many Jews it has turned inward in the form of self-hatred. Elie Wiesel states that Hitler's purpose was the moral and physical destruction of an entire tribe of people. No one was meant to survive. The individual was torn from his milieu, his family, and his past and deprived of his strength, dignity, and memory. By diminishing him and compelling him to see himself through the eyes of his enemy, he thus became his own enemy, hating himself and even wishing his own death. Wiesel illustrates the concept of Jewish self-hatred by a traditional custom: at the end of a meal, one must remove the last knife from the table before reciting the customary blessing that evokes the Jew's yearning for Jerusalem. The reason for this is because the table symbolizes the altar, from which all murderous tools must be removed, and because the Jew must not succumb to the impulse to destroy himself. It appears to be a painful irony that as Jews were chased from country to country, their sages assassinated and their schoolchildren massacred, they have still praised the inviolate sanctity of life even while veiling self-hate.[1]

Wiesel has explored what it means to be a Jew in order to explain this concept of self-hate. To be a Jew means to live with memory and continuity. On the morning of Shavuoth, the Jew feels that he is with Moses receiving the law; on the eve of Tishah b'Av, the Jew weeps together with Rabbi Yohanan Ben-Zakkai over the city of Jerusalem that had been thought indestructible; during the week of Hanukkah, the Jew rushes to the aid of the Maccabees; on Purim, he laughs with Mordecai and celebrates his victory over Haman; and each week, as the wine is blessed over the Sabbath meal, he accompanies his ancestors out of Egypt—forever leaving Egypt, forever having to free himself from bondage.[2]

If the Jews had not transmitted the law to other nations, if the literature of Maimonides, Rashi, Spinoza, Bergson, Einstein, and Freud were nonexistent, if there were no record of the contributions of the Jews to mankind, one thing cannot be contested: history's greatest killers—Pharoah, Nero, Stalin, Hitler—were not Jews. Yet historians have pointed out that self-righteousness has bred self-hating Jews who have been neither authentic nor tolerant and who have provoked anti-Semitism. At the same time, historians were still questioning why neither Hitler nor Rimmler was ever excommunicated by their church; why Auschwitz and Treblinka were never condemned by Pope Pius XII; and why members of the Nazi S.S. remained faithful to their Christian ties to the end.

Chapter 4 – Jewish Self-Hatred

To be a Jew is to express extraordinary contradictions. It means observing Sabbath when the official day of rest is Sunday or Friday. It means studying the Talmud with its seemingly antiquated laws and discussions while outside of the study area, or yeshiva, family members are beaten in a pogrom. These contradictions can foster self-hate at the same time as they foster anti-Semitism.

Jews have always expressed a thirst for knowledge concerning their heritage: Abraham's covenant, the revelation at Sinai, Moses' blessings, the need for pilgrimages to the temple in Jerusalem, Isaiah's words, Talmudic legends, ancient memories and debates, tales of prophets and miracles, litanies about the crusades and the pogroms. Jews have read and reread descriptions of what inquisitors inflicted upon their ancestors. When they turned away from the rites and canons and yet needed to depend on the tolerance of others, they had to know that they were clearly resented.

Persecution and envy imposed in a climate of terror on a frightened community could easily lead to insecurity or self-hate among Jews. The more the Jews were haunted, the more they attempted to rationalize their behavior. Nevertheless, feelings of rejection and distrust had to be recognized, and they sometimes surfaced as self-hate.

The Jews have questioned why there has always been persecution for them in history and for what crimes. What misdeed deserved the many mass graves of the Holocaust? Why was Jerusalem reduced to ashes and plundered? Wiesel suggests that it was because sages and scholars had lost respect and that people were filled with self-hate.

As an example of self-hate, survivors of persecution often feel unworthy to have survived when so many others did not. "Survivors in our time have that in common. They live in constant fear of not knowing how to weep, of being unable to truly weep. They feel that their survival is nothing but an injustice."[3]

The prominence of Jews in the early socialist movement in Europe was a reflection of their long-standing concern for social justice and still another basis for self-hate and pervasive anti-Semitism.[4] By the third quarter of the nineteenth century; Jews had won political equality in nearly every western European country. Just as the Industrial Revolution created capitalist entrepreneurs, it also brought into being a huge proletarian population, concentrated in the larger cities, who soon developed a keen class consciousness. Large numbers of Jews in the laboring groups shared the hazards and insecurities of their fellow workers. Many came to feel that their economic interests were more binding than their religious loyalties. Out of the conflict of labor and capital, a fiercely militant proletarian philosophy emerged in the form of socialism, which sharply attacked the existing order and sought to substitute for it a system of production for use, rather than for profit.

The father of this philosophy, which was destined to change modern history completely, was a dour, plodding, scientific-minded German, Karl Marx, who came from a well-to-do Jewish family. Men of action were required to turn Marx's dialectic into social realities. Among these was the brilliant Jew, Ferdinand Lassalle, who forged the theories of the British Museum bookworm into the powerful social democratic parties of continental Europe.[5]

The fact that Marx and Lassalle sprang from the Jewish group was neither forgotten nor forgiven by anti-Semitic detractors, who inevitably linked all forms of radicalism with the Jews. Yet Marx's family had early converted to Christianity, and young Karl was baptized as an infant and reared in the adopted faith of his parents. Some of his bitterest diatribes were reserved for Jews and Judaism. Later in his life Marx disassociated himself completely from Jewish life, refusing to have anything to do with Jewish laws, customs, or religious observances. Nevertheless, the Jewish origins of Marx, Lassalle, and other creators of socialism were to play a crucial part in the anti-Semitic movements of modern history.[6]

When Karl Marx gave socialism a new radical framework, anti-Semites were well prepared to label his movement "Jewish Marxism" or "Jewish radicalism," despite the fact that Marx's inspirers and followers were all Gentiles. Marx was a particularly caustic anti-Semite, who considered Jews worshipers of mammon, the very soul of the corrupt capitalism he fought. Marx's self-hatred gave ammunition for the economic and cultural kinds of anti-Semitism that were to flourish.

Clearly, Jewish self-hatred has at times aided the forces of anti-Semitism. Once again, however, it is evident that this factor is primarily a product of pre-existing anti-Semitism, and therefore it is grossly unfair to use it to justify anti-Jewish prejudice.

NOTES

[1] Elie Wiesel, *A Jew Today* (New York: Random House, 1978), p. 21.
[2] Ibid., p. 6.
[3] Ibid., p. 23.
[4] Frederick Schweitzer, *A History of the Jews* (New York: Macmillan, 1971), p. 208.
[5] Ibid., p. 207.
[6] Edward H. Flannery, *The Anguish of the Jews* (New York: Macmillan, 1965), p. 166.

Chapter 5: Alleged Jewish Power and Nazi Anti-Semitism

"But thou shalt remember the LORD thy God: for it is he that giveth thee power to get wealth, that he may establish his covenant which he sware unto thy fathers, as it is this day"
(Deuteronomy 8:18).

Another possible contributing factor to anti-Semitism has been Jewish power and the alleged abuse of it over Gentiles. Hitler and the Nazis in particular used this rationale to promote persecution of the Jews, culminating in the Holocaust. In discussing this issue, then, it is instructive to review the prewar history of anti-Semitism in Germany.

Nurtured in the tradition of the rationalist philosophers, Jews were against denominational education and the idea of a state officially dominated by a sect or creed. The Catholic Church denounced this position as a Jewish conspiracy. Political, economic, and religious factors, all operating together, were at the root of anti-Semitism. As one writer states, the fallacies of anti-Semitism could not be argued against, nor the fears dissipated, for anti-Semitism was not a reason, it was a disease.[1]

In Germany, Wilhelm Marr's *Victory of Judaism Over Germanism*, denounced the influence of Jews in the commercial life of Germany and spearheaded a literary furor. When Bismarck repealed anti-Catholic legislation, he skillfully used the Jews as his scapegoats, and Pope Pius IX celebrated Christmas of 1872 by issuing a diatribe accusing the Jews as enemies of Christ. The leading nationalist historian, von Treitschke, proclaimed, "The Jews are our misfortune."[2] Germany was ringing with venomous denunciations. Cultured Germany, a great center of learning, had only to take a short step from discrimination to violence.

After the end of World War I, the unified German nation was a defeated state for the first time in many years. The amazing inequities of the Versailles Treaty that ended the war sought to punish the German nation severely; it was written by some of the most vindictive politicians on the Allied side.

> The provisions of the Versailles Treaty came as a shock to every German. The Germans had expected a treaty freely negotiated along the lines of President Wilson's Fourteen Points, but they were never involved in the actual drafting of the treaty.... [It] was based on the assumption that Germany had intentionally started World War I, and it was intended to

prevent Germany from ever reemerging as a military or political power.

Winston Churchill called the Versailles Treaty a "sad and complicated idiocy." Its effects on Europe and Germany were long reaching and were not what the treaty's makers had intended.

> Germany was forced to pay extensive reparations to the victors, which became a permanent economic, psychological and political burden that hindered efforts at stabilizing the new democracy.... The Versailles Treaty, frustrations with the ineffectiveness of the Weimar government, and pressure by the victors to compel rapid German demobilization set off a series of events in 1920 that almost destroyed the republic within a year after its birth. In March, the so-called Kapp *Putsch* forced President Friedrich Ebert and the legal Weimar government to flee from Berlin.[3]

This was a right-wing coup led by General Walther von Luttwitz and Wolfgang Kapp, and it almost succeeded. It was stopped by a general strike by labor unions and the Social Democratic Party. So we see that the Weimar government was never a stable force in internal German politics. What came from the first anti-Weimar agitation was a basic weakness in central government. It manifested itself in the many years of political violence that were to follow between the left and right wings in Germany.

The return of normalcy and order desired by most Germans did not follow. The gains made by the right did not satisfy the extremists for whom the republic itself symbolized defeat and betrayal.... [There was] the connection between anti-Semitism and anti-republicanism in the minds of the extreme right. Many on the right charged that the republic was created and controlled by Jews to the detriment of "true" Germans. In their propaganda such rightists frequently referred to Weimar as the "Jew Republic."[4]

The rightists described Jewish political and economic power during this time as "parasitic capitalism" and "menacing Marxism." They alleged that Jewish power was at the root of debilitating liberalism, the Versailles Treaty, inflation, racial corruption, immorality, irreligion, and the hated Weimar Republic.[5]

Humiliated by the loss of World War I and crushed by reparations imposed by the Versailles Treaty, Germany was plagued by an economic depression that led to the disastrous inflation of 1923. The middle class was ruined, and unemployment was widespread and chronic. The instrument formed to cope with this deeply troubled period was the liberal Weimar Republic, which became known as the "Jew Republic," since its constitution was drawn up by Hugo Preuss, a powerful Jew. He even managed to abolish the old imperial ban on Jews in public office and to place into the position of foreign minister the efficient and powerful Walter Rathenau, also a Jew. The prominence attained by these powerful leaders among the highly integrated German Jewry led to the charge of domination and overrepresentation by rabid nationalists and growing anti-Semites.

Rathenau's family had built up the A.E.G., the most valuable electrotechnical enterprise in Europe, and at the start of World War I, Rathenau had been in charge of the Department of War Materials, making possible the four years of German resistance. As minister of reconstruction in 1921, he had negotiated the treaty with France; he had also negotiated an advantageous economic agreement with Russia that opened vast potentialities for Russian-German cooperation. As foreign minister, Rathenau held the highest office ever attained by a Jew in Germany, and in June 1922 he was assassinated by six pistol shots from Nazi guns.[6]

The assassination stemmed most directly from two factors. Rathenau's father, Emil, had been the powerful head of the A.E.G. cartel and a close personal friend to Kaiser William II; he even had a special direct telephone line to him. Emil Rathenau was the basis for the claim that the Kaiser had been "politically ruled by the German Department of the Pan-Judaic state."[7] The influence of the Jews and their emergence in leading positions, as represented in turn by Walter Rathenau, was alleged to have forced a peace of unconditional surrender, coordinated by the Jewish central government in London. This was the infamous myth of the "Jewish stab in the back."[8]

The second factor leading to Rathenau's assassination was the *Protocols of the Elders of Zion*, the notorious forgery discussed in chapter 2. It took the form of a dialogue in hell between Machiavelli and Montesquieu, and Machiavelli's words were put into the mouth of the representatives of Judaism. It was even presented as an excerpt from the minutes of the first Zionist Congress of 1897, founded by Theodor Herzl. Zionism, the movement to reestablish the nation of Israel, had been born because of Herzl's despair over the failure of the Jews to achieve equality by assimilation.

The *Protocols* asserted that three hundred wise men of Zion controlled the fate of the world and was interpreted to symbolize Jewish power. Walter Rathenau was considered to be one of the "wise men" by the German National Trutz, the Federation of Frontline Soldiers, the Young German Order, and the University Ring of German Ways. These groups were forerunners of the Nazi regime that were consumed with irrational hatred of Jews. They flooded the press with the contention that Rathenau wanted to destroy Germany and establish Jewish world rule and that his power was "treasonable" and "corrupt."[9]

Dr. Adler points out how Germans felt that they were being influenced by Jewish power: Marx represented the left; Lasker, Preuss, and Rathenau represented the center; and Frederick Stahl, who had proclaimed "the only hindrance to the political equality of the Jews is the Christian character of the state" as he fought for civic power, was on the right. However, Adler shows that in the nineteen governments of the Republic up to 1933, Preuss and Rathenau were the only Jewish Reich ministers out of a total of 387 and that from among 500 civil servants of the Reich with the rank of chief councilor up to secretary of state, there were only 15 Jews. Yet the press spread the word that Germany was ruled by the secret Jewish government, Jewish power in "world finance," and alleged Jewish domination in trade and press.

In actuality, Hugenberg, a German Gentile, controlled more than half of Germany's newspapers, which constituted more than twice the combined holdings of the Jewish firms Mosse and Ullstein since 1919.[10] By 1934, the Nazi press included ten daily newspapers and fifteen weeklies. Headed by Max Amann, the Nazis bought out Ullstein's *Vossisch Zeitung*, comparable to the *New York Times*, without any competitive bid after 230 years of continuous publication. Mosse was forced to surrender his interest in *Frankurter Zeitung*, and the Nazi state's publishing firm, Eher Verlag, became the most lucrative in the world. In 1933 radio, a monopoly owned and operated by the state, automatically came into the possession of the Nazis' Reich Broadcasting Corporation as a chief instrument of propaganda under Goebbels. Films were moved from the control of liberal Jews to Wilhelm Frick, minister of the interior.

Jews were forbidden to teach, and German public schools and universities were brought under the iron rule of the Reich minister of education. Teachers had to take the oath of loyalty and obedience to Adolf Hitler. Famous teachers such as Einstein and Franck were fired, and their influence was discounted as an "instrument of Jewry for the destruction of Nordic science and Aryan thought." The worldwide acclaim Einstein received on the publication of his theory of relativity was denounced by virulent nationalists in *Jewry and Science* as rejoicing over the coming "Jewish world rule which [will] force down German manhood irrevocably." Yet, from 1905 to 1931, ten German Jews had been awarded Nobel Prizes in science.[11]

Crucial targets for anti-Semitism were the financial empires founded by Albert Ballin, Jewish director of the world's largest steamship company, the Hamburg-American Line, and Sir Ernest Cassel, an enormously wealthy Jewish banker with financial ties to the world-famous Jewish House of Rothschild. At the head of commerce and fiscal matters, these families held the reins to powerful decisions.

In 1923, the French and English occupied the industrial belt of Germany known as the Ruhr, which led to the complete collapse of the German economy and the wild "hyperinflation" that drove the mark to become useless paper. Thousands of people were driven to bankruptcy and poverty practically overnight, and this led to increasing political violence by the left and the right.

> All of this [instability] provided opportunities for the extreme right and left. Communist strength in several states increased dramatically, and leftist political violence was just the prelude to a planned Communist revolution. At the same time Bavaria had become a hotbed of right-wing radicalism, which culminated in Hitler's famous Beer Hall *Putsch* of November 8.[12]

Hitler's coup failed, and he was sent to jail, where he wrote *Mein Kampf*, which later came to be the cornerstone of the Nazi Party ideology. Because of the failed *putsch*, Adolf Hitler went from a little-known extremist to

Chapter 5 - Alleged Jewish Power and Nazi Anti-Semitism

a nationally known figure. Both of these events in the key year of 1923 had a profound long-term effect on the future of Germany and Europe.

While the Weimar Republic was failing, the specter of radical anti-Semitism was rising to become a fixed part of German politics. And considering the radical state of confusion and violence that was the norm of that period, it is little wonder that an extreme form of anti-Semitism would come into play. We have already seen that anti-Semitism was always a part of European history and politics. Under the economic stress and chaotic politics of the period, it would seem almost inevitable that those people who considered the Jews an enemy would raise their voices in the almost perpetual search among failing nations for a scapegoat on which to fix the blame for current strife and failures. The Jews, having served this purpose before, did so again in Weimar.

Now we must examine closer the actual anti-Semitism that spread through the unstable Weimar Republic. German anti-Semites claimed that the Jews controlled many institutions such as banks, retail stores, and farms and therefore presented a threat to the German state. To examine these claims a statistical examination of the German Jewish class is necessary. Such a treatment is available in Sarah Gordon's book *Hitler, Germans and the Jewish Question*.

Jews in Germany constituted only 1.09% of the total German population between 1871 and 1933. There were roughly 500,000 Jews by 1933, of which 20% were not native to Germany itself. Jews were more visible because they tended to congregate in larger cities, with one-third of all Jews living in Berlin. In the cities they also tended to live in specific districts or neighborhoods.

Most of the foreign immigrant Jews came from Eastern Europe, and in Germany they continued to follow their Orthodox habits of wearing distinctive black clothing, sidelocks, and yarmulkas. They continued to speak Yiddish and to follow the traditional, Orthodox religious customs. On top of these Jews not being German, these traits placed them even further apart. Moreover, following the Russian Revolution, Jewish immigration to Western Europe grew by some 200,000 in the 1920s. Many of these Jews would then move on to other countries, including America. But many Germans only saw the total numbers of Jews increasing in their country almost daily.[13]

Thus the Jews were a recognizable minority of the German population. Moreover, they did have several specific occupational characteristics that often distinguished them from the other Germans. "They were overrepresented in business, commerce and public and private service; they were underrepresented in agriculture, industry and domestic service."[14]

In 1933 business and commerce had 61% of all Jews in the labor force, compared to 18% of all Germans; 22% of Jews were in industry, 40% of all Germans. Only 2% of the Jews were in agriculture. Jews represented 25% of all individuals in retail businesses and handled 25% of total sales. These were concentrated mostly in such areas as textiles and clothing, grain trading, warehouses, department stores, and metal-related businesses. In banking, Jews were very prominent in both Jewish and non-Jewish firms. Private Jewish banks represented 23% of all banks in 1923 but actually declined to 18% by 1930. In 1930, Jews held 43% of the major positions in private banks; they also held 5.8% of such positions in other banks. In 1913, Jews held 211 seats on boards of directors of banks; by 1928 they held 718 such seats. In the stock market, insurance companies, legal firms, and economic consulting firms, Jews were also prominent, with Jews having 13% of directorships of joint-stock firms, 24% of the supervisory positions in the firms, 3% of the membership in the influential German Economic Council, and 80% of the top positions in the stock exchange—85% by 1933, when the Nazis eliminated them.

Most of the Jews who engaged in blue-collar jobs were the newer immigrants, who held 36% of the Jewish blue-collar jobs and came to represent 23% of all Jews in the work force. Only 1 to 3% of all civil servants were Jewish, and they were found at all levels of civil service. Between 1933 and 1939, the Nazis dismissed 17,375 lawyers, junior barristers, and civil servants because they were Jews.

In the universities, Jews were overrepresented both among professors and students. In 1910 Jews were 12% of instructors, and 7% were Jews converted to Christianity. In 1905-06, 25% of legal and medical students and 34% of philosophy students were Jewish.

In the arts, theater, film and journalism, Jews were highly active. In 1931, 50% of theater directors were Jewish. Of the plays produced in 1930, 75% were written by Jews, and many actors and actresses were Jewish. Jews were very prominent in many facets of what is now known as "Weimar culture." In 1881, 9% of all journalists were Jewish and the number rose by 1933.[16]

These statistics are enough to indicate where the German Jewish minority was located economically. Many were in the highly visible and public occupations such as banking, stock market, retail stores, and buying and selling in general. Jewish artists, actors, writers, and journalists were prominent in Weimer Germany.

These dull but necessary statistics provide a clearer picture of the role of the German Jews.

> If one considers all of the branches of the economy, it is clear that Jews were significantly overrepresented as "independents," that is, a larger percentage of Jews than non-Jews was self-employed. This reflected not only self-employment of Jews in business and commerce, but also their very considerable numbers in free professions. They were also more highly represented as white-collar workers than the Germans as a whole.[16]

Due to this white-collar visibility, the Jews as a group made more money and thus paid higher taxes than most working Germans.

> This in itself gave the Jewish minority considerable visibility. High incomes were partially a product of the small number of extremely wealthy Jews [and] the large percentage of Jews at middle income levels.... One gains the impression that Jews were more successful in their careers and income than were

non-Jews. It would, however, be a misconception to assume that Jews had a stronghold on the German economy. Jews were never the powerful "captains of industry" who produced the bulk of Germany's manufactured goods; rather, their roles were predominantly those of middlemen, financiers and members of the free professions and cultural fields.[17]

As Gordon points out, the occupations and positions that most of the German Jews held made it that much easier for the anti-Semites to draw grotesque conclusions about the actual extent of Jewish penetration and control over fields such as arts, banking, journalism, and the civil service. While many Jews were extraordinarily successful and highly visible in society for reasons discussed in chapter 3, nevertheless it is clear that Jews did not control the government or economy of Germany. They were not in a position to exercise great abusive power over Gentiles, and the Nazi charge that they did is irrational and unfounded. The major effect of this ludicrous charge was to rally disenchanted Germans to the Nazi cause and to consolidate the power of the Nazi party.

Let us examine this Nazi claim to see how it came about and how it was used. First, we must understand how the Nazis came to power as a political group. They had tried and failed in the abortive Beer Hall *Putsch* of 1923, and Hitler and the other leaders were jailed. But Hitler served only nine months and was soon freed to continue agitation in the chaotic and increasingly violent Weimar world. The Nazis were one of many radical parties, as were the Socialists and Communists. Political ideology aside, these groups had much in common that appealed to the frightened people of the time: "the paramilitary organization, the exceptionally important role of charismatic leaders... the pseudo-religious, missionary type of propaganda and rhetoric, the high degree of activism exhibited by these movements and their functionaries."[18]

The Nazis had shown their willingness to fight in the Beer Hall *Putsch*; their activism and violence was directed against the Communists, their rhetoric and propaganda was directed against the Jews, and their leader, Adolf Hitler, was indeed charismatic.

An example of their earliest propaganda is cited below. It is translated from a Nazi Party leaflet written by an early Nazi leader and confidant of Adolf Hitler, one Anton Drexler:

> Dear Colleagues: It is a workingman speaking to you-one who still stands at the lathe.... There is a secret world conspiracy, which while speaking much about humanity and tolerance, in reality wants only to harness the people to a new yoke.... 300 big bankers, financiers and press barons, who are inter- connected across the world, are the real dictators.... The Jewish big capitalist always plays our friend and do-gooder.... The trusting worker is going to help him set up the world dictatorship of Jewry.... Comrades, do you want to be Jewish slaves? Bolshevism is a Jewish swindle."[19]

That pamphlet was written in 1920 under the auspices of the newly formed Nazi Party. By 1929, when the

Chapter 5 - Alleged Jewish Power and Nazi Anti-Semitism

Nazis were the largest right-wing party in the Bundestag, their propaganda had changed little from its earliest days:

> German farmers! Farmers, it is a matter of your house and home!... Factories, forests, railways, taxes and the state's finances have all been robbed by the Jew. Insatiable Jewish race-lust and fanaticism are the driving forces behind this devilish attempt to break Germany's backbone.... That same state is totally Jew-ridden in all its organs, and today can be called German in name only. Under the eyes of the so-called authorities the Jew is running a lucrative middleman Stock Exchange.[20]

A careful reading of these and other propaganda from the Nazi era shows an almost complete adherence to all the clichés of anti-Semitism. The Nazis insisted that the "world conspiracy of Jewry" was responsible for all of the ills of economically stricken Germany. Everything was the fault of Jews who could control the prices the farmers got for their crops through their manipulation and control of the stock market.

In every way, the Nazis used the achievements of the Jews in Germany to promote their basic anti-Semitism. In 1932, the Nazis drew more than thirteen million votes, and when Hitler took over the Reichstag, the Jews were not just scapegoats and members of an inferior race but the cause of every problem and the poisoner of Aryan blood. Under the Nazi slogan "Jewry perish!" the "solution to the Jewish problem" was set in motion.[21] Every facet of German life was "de-Judaized." The "Krystallnacht," the night when the Nazis stormed and plundered Jewish businesses, marked the point of no return.

The Nuremberg Laws of September 15, 1935, decreed by the Nazi government, deprived the Jews of German citizenship. These were followed by thirteen additional decrees that excluded Jews from public and private employment to the extent that one-half were without means of livelihood. These laws barred Jews from working in stock exchanges, radio, farming, teaching, theater, or films. What once had been sites of power now displayed taunting signs: "Jews Strictly Forbidden." A national boycott of Jewish shops was in effect from April 1, 1933.[22]

The quavering appeasement twins, Chamberlain and Daladier, who sought "peace in our time," were no match for the obsessive anti-Semitism of Hitler, Goering, Goebbels, Rosenberg, Streicher, Darre, Rimmler, Heydrich, and Eichmann nor the death camps at Chelmo, Maidanek, Treblinka, Belzec, Sobibor, and Auschwitz.

Ultimately, Nazi anti-Semitism resulted in the Holocaust, which surpassed even the bloody crusades of the Middle Ages by the death of six million men, women, and children. The historian must write his summary in the solemn spirit of the *kaddish*, the Jewish prayer for the dead.

Chapter 5 - Alleged Jewish Power and Nazi Anti-Semitism

NOTES

[1] Abram L. Sachar, *A History of the Jews* (New York: Alfred Knopf, 1974), p. 348.
[2] Ibid.
[3] Joseph W. Bendersky, *A History of Nazi Germany* (Chicago: Nelson-Hall Publishing Co., 1985), p. 11.
[4] Ibid., p. 12.
[5] H. G. Adler, *The Jews in Germany* (Indiana: University of Notre Dame Press, 1969), p. 122.
[6] Ibid., p. 123.
[7] Ibid., p. 124.
[8] Frederick Schweitzer, *A History of the Jews* (New York: Macmillan Company, 1971), p. 218.
[9] Ibid., p. 219.
[10] Adler, p. 133.
[11] William Shirer, *The Rise and Fall of the Third Reich* (New York: Simon and Schuster, 1960), p. 251.
[12] Bendersky, p. 13.
[13] Sarah Gordon, *Hitler, Germans and the Jewish Question* (Princeton, N.J.: Princeton University Press, 1984), pp. 8-10.
[14] Ibid., pp. 11-12.
[15] Ibid., pp. 12-14.
[16] Ibid., p. 12.
[17] Ibid., pp. 8-18. The statistics are taken from chapter one of Gordon's book.
[18] Martin Broszat, "National Socialism, Its Social Basis and Psychological Impact," in *Upheaval and Continuity*, ed. by E. J. Feuchtwanger (Pittsburgh: University of Pittsburgh Press, 1974), p. 134.
[19] Simon Taylor, *The Rise of Hitler* (New York: Universe Books, 1983), pp. 63-64.
[20] Ibid., p. 83.
[21] Edward H. Flannery, *The Anguish of the Jews* (New York: Macmillan, 1964), p. 210.
[22] Shirer, p. 204.

Chapter 6: Inadequate Views of the Holocaust

"Thou shalt not hate thy brother in thine heart"
(Leviticus 19: 17).

God's mandate for interpersonal relationships has always been a challenge to fulfill, but one wonders how so many people can look at the traumatic killing of six million men, women, and children in a detached manner, with little or no compassion.

What did happen to the six million Jews who were said to have been exterminated during World War II? Morally deranged and spiritually perverted pseudo-historians have written and lectured that the Holocaust never took place. Paul Rassinier, a pioneer of the revisionist approach, reflects on "The Lie of Auschwitz. Did Six Million Really Die? The Truth at Last." Austin J. App, chairman of the Department of English at LaSalle College in Philadelphia, published "The Six Million Swindle: blackmailing the German people for hard marks with fabricated corpses." Anne Frank's *Diary of a Young Girl* was termed a forgery by an ambassador at the United Nations. The president of the German-American Committee of Greater New York, a cultural organization with fifty branches in the metropolitan area, objected that there is no real proof that the Holocaust actually did happen. The academic community did not boycott Northwestern University professor Arthur Butz when he called it the "hoax of the century," claiming that the Nuremberg trials and the Frankfurt trials were never held, there was no "selection," Mengele was just another physician, Eichmann merely a bureaucrat, and Hitler never intended to exterminate the Jews.

Challenging these publications, Elie Weisel has stated, "The ultimate viciousness appears to be to try to make people believe—and many already do—that the death factories of Chelmno, Maidanek, Belzec, Janowska, Auschwitz, Buchenwald, Babi Yar, Treblinka, and Birkenau never existed."[1] He points out that from late 1942 on *The New York Times* gave full coverage and printed detailed plans of the Final Solution. Daring inmates inside Auschwitz succeeded in photographing hell and in smuggling photographs out to Cracow, where they were transmitted to London and on to Washington. Nevertheless, when Allied leaders were asked to bomb the railroad tracks leading to Birkenau, where day after day more than ten thousand Jews were exterminated during a period, they categorically refused. If the Allied headquarters did not consider rescuing Jews from death worth the effort or the risk and if not one commander shifted his troops in order to liberate this or that camp ahead of schedule, then why should the display of detachment of other Gentiles be amazing? Weisel asks.[2]

The great majority of Holocaust survivors from Central Europe had no homes or families to go to. Trampled men, humiliated women and lonely adolescents vegetated for years in camp barracks designated for "displaced persons," and were considered subhumans. (Nobody had really wanted them in prewar Germany either.) The gates of Palestine, still under British mandate, were shut. As in the thirties, the United States distributed visas only to the healthy, productive candidates. Refugees with the gravest problems were welcomed by Norway, but this was a small country with limited resources. With the exception of salaried officials of specialized international organizations, survivors, who once had been more accustomed to give than to receive, were thought to be incapable of dignity. They were thought to be born vagrants. The war was over for everybody except for them. They were usually treated condescendingly as ill-adjusted children. Not one survivor was asked to be a member of the special council in charge of the financial reparations negotiations with West Germany. Not one survivor sat on the international council of the famous claims conference. The consensus was that they were recluses, misfits, intruders, and carriers of disease. They began to feel superfluous in a society that continued to repudiate them.[3]

There have been novels, films, plays, and documentaries about the Holocaust, but the term "Holocaust literature" appears to be a contradiction. How can one communicate that which by its very nature defies language? The great novelists of the period did not grapple with this theme covered by ashes that could evoke guilt among the living. It is far easier to view such a situation with detached objectivity than with heart-rending compassion.

It appears that Gentiles need to think of the Holocaust as only an accident of history. The height of irony and cruelty were the brutal questions that they often intrusively posed to survivors: "Why did you survive? Was it because you were more cunning, hardier, tenacious, selfish? Why are you commercializing on your experience?"[4]

The American Jewish Committee has emphasized that teaching about the Holocaust is an important way of combatting anti-Semitism among millions of American schoolchildren. This concern led to a 1979 study by Dr. Glenn Pate at the University of Arizona. The study examined in detail 43 textbooks that represented virtually all the major sources of information in history and social science available to students through textbook publishers in America. Out of the 43 books, only five devoted as much as 40 lines to the Holocaust.[5] Dr. Bruno Bettlehiem analyzed the results of Dr. Pate's study and emphasized that most books give a few facts of what happened without any serious attempt to explain why the events occurred. Only few texts in use in schools present a fuller version of the Holocaust within its historical context and setting.

There are a number of psychological reasons that may explain why many Gentiles can regard the Holocaust with apparent equanimity. These share a base in so-called escape techniques by which most individuals seek to avoid

Chapter 6 - Inadequate Views of the Holocaust

feelings of discomfort, tension, and pain. One such mechanism is "rationalization," which can work in several ways. The "rational" Gentile might claim that his particular ethnic or religious group has also suffered through the ages. Blacks cite the rigors of slavery, Armenians the massacre of perhaps millions at the hands of the Turks, Russians and Poles their fate during the Nazi era. What then, they ask, makes the Jewish situation so special or unique?[6]

Attempts to rationalize the Holocaust are assisted as well by the natural tendency to focus on the here and now, a process greatly accelerated by the mass media. Every day seems to bring new and fresh disasters to rend our hearts and minds. With so much tragedy at hand, why retrogress into past events that we can do nothing to prevent or rectify? It is healthier, say many psychiatrists, to forget the past and to live for the present. We must "get on" with our lives and let the dead bury the dead, as it were. Surely, this "realistic response" to those who seek to keep the memory of the Holocaust alive aids in the development of Gentile indifference or even boredom with the topic.[7]

Another relevant phenomenon in today's society is the "blame-the-victim" syndrome, which a number of psychologists have identified. Thus, the rape victim is somehow at fault in the crime committed against her, the poor are held responsible for their poverty, and by the same thought process, the Jews are held accountable, at least in part, for the Holocaust.

Various arguments are advanced for this astounding belief structure. For example, Hitler warned the Jews to leave Germany, but they did not. Of course, this view fails to emphasize the immorality of Hitler's threat or to list which nations were willing to accept any refugees who would respond to the Nazi "invitation." Similarly, Gentiles vaguely mention that the Jews must have done something to arouse the ire of the Germans, by more wealth, better jobs, education, or whatever set them apart for "special treatment." Moreover, Jewish "councils" established by the Nazis in occupied lands had the duty of selecting those in their ghetto communities who would be transported—to their deaths as events transpired. These and other instances are given to illustrate the seeming culpability of the Jews in their own destruction and allow many non-Jews a good deal of composure in contemplating the Holocaust.[8]

But we must not allow any of these psychological mechanisms to obscure the plain truth. The Holocaust did in fact occur, and while most Gentiles alive today cannot be held accountable for it, they are morally obligated to keep its memory alive so that it will never happen again. The goal of every rational, moral person should be the elimination of all vestiges of anti-Semitism as well as all other forms of prejudice.

Chapter 6 - Inadequate Views of the Holocaust

NOTES

[1] Elie Weisel, *A Jew Today* (New York: Random House, 1978), p.

[2] Ibid., p. 19.

[3] Dr. Sidney Tarachow, "A Note on Anti-Semitism," *Psychiatry* IX (1946), p. 60.

[4] Tarachow, p. 62.

[5] Ernest Volkman, *A Legacy of Hate, Anti-Semitism in America* (New York: Franklin Watts Co., 1982), p. 193.

[6] G. F. Mahl, *Psychological Conflict and Defense* (New York: Harcourt, Brace, Jovanovich, 1971), pp. 18-36.

[7] F. Heider, *The Psychology of Interpersonal Relationships* (New York: Wiley, 1963), pp. 112-17.

[8] Tamotsu Shibutani, *Society and Personality* (Englewood Cliffs, N.J.: Prentice-Hall, 1966), pp. 181-95.

Chapter 7:
Remembering the Holocaust

Many people, both Jews and Gentiles, would like to put the tragedy of the Holocaust behind them and forget the past. However, some experts believe that frequent remembrance of the Holocaust acts as a deterrence to anti-Semitism. Far from viewing the darkest chapter of Jewish history as a mechanism for bolstering resentment against the Jews, some authorities feel that the Holocaust and the events surrounding it help prevent anti-Semitism today.

> Until the Holocaust, enemies of the Jews, whether pagans, Christians, Muslims, men of the Enlightenment, Leftists, or Nazis, proudly and publicly espoused their opposition to the Jews. Since the revelations of the Nazi crimes, however, it has become taboo to call oneself an opponent of the Jews, and today, for the first time in history, antisemitics deny that they are antisemitic. In fact, contemporary anti-

semites often go one step further and insist that they actually like Jews.... If one is to take such people by their words, there are no more antisemites on the face of the earth.... Since the revelations of the Holocaust the most hated people in history have no longer a single enemy.[1]

Certainly, even the most ardent proponent of the idea that the Holocaust and the memories it evokes have somehow served to make Jews "better liked" or at least "more tolerated" would not claim that this event killed anti-Semitism in all times and places in the recent past. But it seems likely that the Holocaust has indeed functioned to mitigate the more virulent strain of anti-Semitism, especially in America and in Europe, which gave birth to the mentality that allowed the attempted erasure of a population group. Surely some degree of guilt is aroused in Gentiles when the subject of the Holocaust is brought to their attention; this may be greater or lesser in a given individual, of course.

It should be borne in mind that neither the United States nor any other Western nation wanted to take in those Jews subject to Nazi persecution before the Final Solution. Hitler began quite modestly, only wishing to be rid of the Jews of Germany. When no country proved willing to accept these possible refugees, he apparently felt rather justified in taking further steps. It was evident that, despite high-flown rhetoric in the democratic states about the excesses of the Nazi regime, no one wanted "extra" Jews no matter what their eventual fate might be. After that fate became public knowledge, consciences were perhaps sore; in the United States and England this feeling took the form of support for a Jewish state where Jews would once and forever be free of persecution.

Once this "magnanimous" step was taken, however, it is debatable whether or not people felt more must be done to remove those uncomfortable feelings of guilt over the Holocaust. Any lingering feelings of guilt are likewise tempered by the discovery that many important American Jewish leaders had, prior to the actual outbreak of World War II, been silent on the issue of bringing German Jews, particularly 20,000 children, to the United States. The question is still asked—certainly by those harboring anti-Semitic leanings—Where were the American Jews while the six million died? Research has also disclosed offers by certain Zionists to collaborate with Nazi Germany. Guilt is mitigated when the Jews themselves can be perceived as also at fault in the wake of the Holocaust.[2]

Constant reminders of the Holocaust, whether in the media, by churches and other organizations, or in the educational process, serve to keep the event alive to new generations. For example, Jewish leaders hope that textbooks will highlight how a crime of greatest magnitude could have occurred among civilized people and thereby help to prevent any historical repeat. The hope is that as young people try to understand the horror of hatred and prejudice so deep that it could lead to the murder of millions, they will be deterred from anti-Semitic thoughts and deeds.

It is possible, however, that continual references to the Holocaust could cause a backlash, creating effects quite different from what American Jewish policymakers desire. As an inkling of this possibility, many non-Jews in both America and Germany are beginning to express doubts about the further prosecution of responsible Nazis found in the United States. We hear comments that too much time has elapsed, that these people have led respectable lives for years, that they are too old to be punished now. In other words, we should allow the past to die quietly.

Certainly, American Jews, assisted by the sympathy aroused by the Holocaust, have been successful in halting any major acts of anti-Semitism in the United States since World War II. Indeed, the tragedy has generated support for Israel among non-Jews, even when this backing has at times conflicted with American self interests. Among anti-Semitic elements, however, the oil boycott, higher prices, and longer lines for gasoline—to offer one example—did not go unnoted. They blamed the Jews and the American politicians who consistently supported Israel for hurting Americans in the pocketbook.

The Holocaust has helped Soviet Jews to gain backing. However, even before the rise of those revisionists of history who deny that the Holocaust ever took place, Soviet books and films on the period virtually ignored it to the point of denying it. For example, a nearly hour-long film shown to Russian visitors to Auschwitz, Poland—where more than three million Jews were killed—makes no mention of the Jews. The Soviets have gone further, using the Holocaust as a vehicle to increase anti-Semitism by depicting Zionists as actively working with the Nazis in the death camps. They say that Jews, while admittedly Nazi prisoners, worked under their masters to kill brave

Russian soldiers of war. Thus the Soviets try to link Nazism to Zionism.[3]

There are certain risks in utilizing the Holocaust as a vehicle against anti-Semitism. There is the danger of overkill: the repeated message of the tragedy could grow stale, grow boring, or become trivialized through exposure. Some Gentiles see the Holocaust as Jewish propaganda, something Jews emphasize whenever Israel wants to make demands on the American Congress or when the United Nations condemns Israeli treatment of the Palestinians, for example. This complaint is not the same as denial of the Holocaust itself, of course. However, a heavy-handed play of the Holocaust merely invites people to attempt some form of revisionism. Just as a mountain is there to climb, presenting a perpetual challenge, so is the Holocaust to some historians. For them it is difficult to resist the challenge of debunking such an infamous, horrendous episode in the annals of man—a memory kept so much alive.

Jewish-American leaders have correctly assessed the popular mood among Gentiles: sympathy, guilt, and pity for the slaughter of a people. As with other tragic events, however, the Holocaust remains ever fresh to those directly affected, but to others the message tends to diminish with time, despite on-going appeals. But we must not allow society to forget the lessons of the Holocaust or to relegate it to just another page in a dusty history book.

On the other hand, Jewish leaders and friends of the Jews should not complacently assume that they can always rely upon this mechanism to stem future outbreaks of anti-Semitic activity for all time. The ability of Jewish leaders to utilize the media to keep the Holocaust before the general public prompts some comment on the prominence of Jews in this sphere of American life—the idea that they have the power to manipulate opinion in ways favorable to themselves. While the Holocaust was, and remains, a potent weapon for combatting anti-Semitism, that weapon can become a two-edged sword that turns against those who wield it unwisely.

NOTES

[1] Dennis Prager and Joseph Telushkin, *Why the Jews?: The Reason for Antisemitism* (New York: Simon & Schuster, 1983), pp. 169.

[2] Henry Feingold, *The Politics of Rescue* (New Brunswick, N.J.: Rutgers University Press, 1970), pp. 215- 19.

[3] Prager and Telushkin, pp. 144-45.

Chapter 8: Anti-Semitism in America Today

History repeats itself, but could something so monstrously demonic as the Holocaust be repeated? We all pray that it could never happen again, but some similarities do exist now between America and prewar Germany.

Chicago Tribune articles of September 8, 1985, reported about neo-Nazis who have targeted Jews and bankers for assassination. A commando squad of 23 neo-Nazis planned to assassinate successful and prominent Jewish figures, including media executives and bankers, before virtually its entire membership was arrested. Individuals they targeted for murder included former Secretary of State Henry Kissinger, French banker Baron Phillipe Rothschild, Denver talk-show host Alan Berg (whom they later did murder), the presidents of the ABC, CBS, and NBC television networks, and Chase Manhattan

Bank chief David Rockefeller, according to the testimony of Denver Daw Parmenter, a member of the neo-Nazi group called the Order. The Order was linked to three armored-car robberies, two bank robberies, and a sophisticated counterfeiting scheme that together netted nearly four million dollars in less than six months. The money was used to buy weapons and supplies for future crimes and to donate to other groups in "the white movement against Jews."[1]

History teaches that every outbreak of anti-Semitism has a later, tragic echo, as German Jews discovered. The status of the Jewish community in America is disturbingly similar to the situation in Weimar Germany. As in Weimar, the Jewish community has enjoyed power and prestige. When the first great wave of anti-Semitism struck in Germany, the Jewish community was divided, confused, and bereft of allies, and it finally perished. Regrettably, a similar state of confusion exists today in the modern American Jewish community. Jews are uncertain about the direction of the new anti-Semitism, confused over what to do about it, and at cross-purposes about the loss of their allies on the left and in the black community. Simply put, American Jews no longer seem to know who the enemy is, and in their groping for answers, they have entered what may be a great period of danger in their history, especially considering some of the stresses and strains tearing at the fabric of the American Jewish community from inside.[2]

Anti-Semitism concentrates on accusing the Jews of being... Jews. The Jews are fundamentally "other." That otherness has been the focus of anti-Semitism for centuries: Hellenistic anti-Semites were infuriated by the Jews'

Chapter 8 - Anti-Semitism in America Today

hostility toward the pantheon of Greek gods, Christian anti-Semites were angered by the Jewish refusal to accept the new light, and modern anti-Semites object to what they see as a dangerous sociopolitical entity. For this reason, anti-Semitism is not an abstraction to Jews, who tend to be alert for the slightest tremors like the first wavering of lines on a seismograph that signal the approach of an earthquake.[3]

Samuel Van Pelt, a former circuit court judge and a consultant on the subject of anti-Semitism to the governor of Nebraska, Bob Kerry, warned, "What we are seeing in the Farm Belt in America is not unlike what happened in Germany when Hitler got his start. Hitler started with a few disillusioned people, who found the Jews a handy scapegoat, and built it into a Nazi empire. Now we see some very clever people trying to do the same thing with our beleaguered farmers."[4]

Van Pelt described the "Battle of the Wheatfields," in which hundreds of automatic weapons, more than 200,000 rounds of ammunition, $125,000 worth of stolen farm equipment, and rustled cattle were confiscated by Nebraskan authorities from two thousand ultrarightists who preached to debt-ridden farmers. They advocated violent anti-Semitism and falsely proclaimed that farmers' loans were being called because a cabal of Jewish bankers was working behind the scenes to cripple the American economy. Thus a dark, new element emerged in the American farm crisis: a grass-roots Nazi movement in the heartland.

Researcher Charles Silberman expresses a more optimistic view. He asserts that the descendants of the Jews who fled repression, poverty, and pogrom have, in less than 150 years and especially since World War II, entered "the mainstream of American life." In politics, especially since 1960, Jews "are being elected to every kind of position, by every kind of constituency, in every part of the country." Citing Irving Shapiro, a former chairman of DuPont, as an example, he notes that long-closed doors in industry have opened as anti-Semitism has declined. Silberman points out that major, positive social and cultural breakthroughs for American Jews have occurred since World War II and that a person's position depends largely on what he can do rather than on who he is.[5]

Silberman stresses that America today is rejecting anti-Semitism and that America now places no limit on American Jewry in its pursuit of temporal success. He feels that Jews are now able to express their Jewishness without inhibiting their full participation in American life, and unlike prewar Germany, this revitalization is a strengthening force. Silberman finds the current intermarriage rate to be about twenty-eight percent, not the forty or sixty percent frequently mentioned by others. "The overwhelming majority of American Jews are choosing to remain Jews, unlike what occurred in pre-war Germany," he asserts.[6]

For Silberman, the success of Jewish life in America is due to the belief that there is "a mysterious and awesome relationship between God and the Jewish people, and there is a conviction, in some incomprehensible way, that what happens to the Jewish people affects the fate of the world." He suggests that the answer lies in an America that rejects anti-Semitism because it has found enough strength and unity in its diversity, unlike prewar Germany, to place no limit on American Jewry.[7]

The outpouring of anti-Semitic rhetoric from Black Muslim leader Louis Farrakhan at rallies across America placed another element into the equation in 1985. His opinions were given the aura of religious certitude and were injected into public discourse as fact. He twinned himself with Jesus Christ portraying both as victims of persecution by Jews.

To invoke the name of Jesus in an attack on Jews appears to be a denial of the very compassion for which the Prince of Peace is worshiped, just as to inveigh against New York as the "capital city of Jews" appeals to mindlessness. Farrakhan referred to Judaism as a "gutter religion," dubbed a Washington Post reporter a "Judas who shall be punished with death," and termed Hitler a great man, but he was invited to be the guest speaker at the National Press Club in Washington and was presented with a certificate of appreciation. Farrakhan was joined by Jesse Jackson in broadcasts and lectures that called for black economic opportunity and self-reliance, but this message has been largely drowned out by the roar of bigotry.

Some public figures have spoken out against the anti-Semitism generated, but others fall back on the argument that silence is the best policy, perhaps failing to realize that answering anti-Semitic rhetoric with silence is tantamount to condoning it. Historian H.G. Adler has asserted, "The most dangerous medium of anti-Semitic propaganda is broadcasting, as it completes the unhindered education of the people in the spirit of acid hatred for the Jews. The rise of the Nazi party in Germany took place with a parallel awareness of the National Socialism Program, and the hatred for the Jews." 8

Jews in America today enjoy freedom and opportunity to a degree perhaps unparalleled in their history, but even so the threat of anti-Semitism remains. People of good will everywhere must continue to speak out against this and all other racism.

NOTES

[1] James Coates, *Chicago Tribune*, September 8, 1985.
[2] Ernest Volkman, *A Legacy of Hate, Anti-Semitism in America* (New York: Franklin Watts Co., 1982), p. 6.
[3] Ibid., p. 8
[4] James Coates, *Chicago Tribune*, September 26, 1985.
[5] Charles Silberman, *A Certain People* (New York: Summit Books, 1985), p. 124.
[6] Ibid., p. 140.
[7] Ibid., p. 165.
[8] H.G. Adler, *The Jews in Germany* (Indiana: University of Notre Dame Press, 1969), p. 134.

Chapter 9: Combatting Anti-Semitism

"And the LORD appeared unto him the same night, and said, I am the God of Abraham thy father: fear not, for I am with thee, and will bless thee, and multiply thy seed for my servant Abraham's sake" (Genesis 26: 24).

These words are comforting but nevertheless fears exist in the Jewish community that another Holocaust, if not probable, is in fact possible. And lesser manifestations of anti-Semitism still occur in our world.

"By far the most common Jewish response to anti-Semitism [since the Holocaust]... is to fight it whenever it erupts and attempt to identify and suppress its source before it erupts." Organizations such as the Anti-Defamation League of the B'nai B'rith and the American Jewish Committee have "vigilantly monitored the far Right and Left for signs of anti-Semitism and have generally effectively silenced Jew-haters through public exposure." Jews have learned to utilize the media in their own best interests and have used their undoubted political power to place in office those sympathetic to the Jewish need to fight against both domestic and foreign enemies of the Jewish people.[1]

It is apparent that the Jews believe that "it" can happen again... and happen here. Given the overall success of Jewish organizations and individuals in winning support for Jewish rights and causes in America and for the nation of Israel, why should the Jewish community acknowledge such fears at least tacitly, if not openly? Let us seek some possible answers.

There are several theories as to why a cycle of persecution of Jews arises periodically. Although the Holocaust was unique in its scope, the reasons for its appearance, as well as for pogroms throughout history, are not. Time after time, in locations ranging over much of the earth's expanse, various people have desired to eradicate at least some portion of this singled-out group. Jewish organizations therefore have no cause to believe that such feelings will not spring up once more, even in the United States.

One theory for the appearance of holocausts, large and small, is that difficult periods of economic and social strain induce a need to find a scapegoat—someone or some group to blame for the ills of the total society. This factor has, of course, been frequently cited in the case of Nazi Germany. Given a second depression of major proportions in the United States, the Jews might draw a great share of blame for the collapse, especially when the financial apparatus that undergirds the economic structure is widely held to be under the control of Jews. Nor could the Jewish community necessarily look to political officials, whom they themselves might have aided in the attainment of power, for it might well be politically expedient for these non-Jewish politicians to go along with majority desires, attacking the Jews as the source of disaster.[2]

Another apparent cause for past pogroms and the Holocaust—and possibly a source of future ones—is racism. Jews have been the target of race hatred in many places and eras. Racists begin to focus on Jews as a target once their number or prominence in a particular area of society brings them to the attention of such groups. For example, before the influx of Eastern European Jews starting in 1881, the Jewish population in the United States was " small, inconspicuous, and highly assimilated." There were too few American Jews "for them to constitute a Jewish problem." But beneath this seemingly inert and peaceful surface, anti-Semitism was far from dead. It only needed the "hordes" of new immigrants, "impoverished, sometimes culturally backward, adherents of pre-modern religious beliefs and customs"—in other words, a highly visible group—to arouse latent race hatred.[3]

That visibility has been a factor in race hatred can be viewed in the most unexpected settings, including the most respected universities in the country. As the children of Jewish immigrants of the turn of the century began attending institutions of higher learning in proportions much larger than the Jewish share of the population, the attention of administration, professors, and non-Jewish students became centered on this "out" group. At Harvard, which had earned a reputation as the "most liberal and democratic of the Eastern schools," one dormitory came to be known as "Little Jerusalem" because many

"Hebes" resided there; a fraternity song stated that "when the little sheenies die, their souls will go to hell."[4]

This is not to imply that Harvard or any other college is a likely spot for a new Holocaust to begin. Rather, this example shows that when a minority group impinges on the attention of even the most "civilized" old guard, there is usually a reaction of resentment. As the Jewish Alumni Society of Harvard noted in the 1920s, "The anti-Semitic feeling among the students is increasing, and it grows in proportion to the increase in the number of Jews. If their number should become 40 percent of the student body, the race feeling would become intense." The president of Harvard found "very great evils for the Jews" because of their visibility and called for "racial quotas" as the way to reduce tensions by making Jews less noticeable on college campuses.[5]

Jewish groups fought against such restrictions on their upward mobility; interestingly, in the recent past, they have incurred the wrath of blacks by their refusal to support affirmative action in a somewhat similar situation. It appears then, that high visibility carries danger with it for a minority group; in certain instances, it can be a cause for persecution, if not an actual Holocaust.

While no pogrom has ever occurred on American soil, an anti-Semitic nationalism has gripped many people in the United States in certain periods of its history; usually these periods of more overt prejudice are times of economic, political, or social stress. One prime example was the Great Depression, an era marked by one group turning against the other. Many Gentiles believed the canard that the economic problems of America were the fault of Jewish international bankers. The rise of fascism, which had its onset about the same time, heightened hatred against the Jews as fears of war increased. Such noted individuals as Henry Ford and Charles Lindberg stated publicly that Jews had manipulated the economy, causing the Depression in order to advance their own wealth and power, or were trying to drag the nation into war to save the Jews of Europe.[6]

Episodes such as this, including present-day charges that Jews are behind financial failures in the agricultural sector, mean that Jewish citizens and their organizations have to be constantly alert to attacks from many directions. Prompt responses to all forms of anti-Semitism may be the primary reason why pogroms have never taken place in America.

This is not to say that an outbreak could never occur in this nation. The old arguments for saying "it can't happen here," rooted in such premises as opportunity for all and religious toleration, have not held true across the broad span of American history. Although success has met the efforts to avoid major outbreaks of anti-Jewish hatred, these exertions have done little to counter the root causes of anti-Semitism but rather have sought the more modest—and attainable—goal of treating indications of its appearance. Many of the more common evidences of hate for the Jews have today lost their outward thrust. That is, name-calling, vandalism of synagogues, and Jew "bashing" have moved out of the range of norms and values of mainstream American society. Certainly, particular groups may voice epithets of the past "off the record" in discussing Jews, but in the more "polite" segments of the culture, this practice is no longer indulged in routinely.

Because Gentiles do not roam the streets shouting derogatory slogans or names does not mean that their hearts and minds are free of all anti-Semitic thoughts. In fact, it is possible to read more danger in the privatization of hatred of the Jews. When feelings are openly expressed, even when those feelings are expressed in violent acts, it is less difficult to meet the challenge; half the battle may be in knowing the enemy. It is difficult for either organizations or individuals to counter the enemy who refuses to acknowledge himself as such. He remains an unknown quantity, but in the shadows of private life he can sow seeds of public outbreak sometime in the future. For instance, the Jewish community as a whole felt for years that the friendliness of black Americans was a certainty. Recently, however, a variety of differences have surfaced between the two groups over affirmative action, the Arabs, and other pressure points. Yet once these problems are aired, it is possible at least to attain compromises, if not solutions. It is when resentments are bottled up that violent outbreaks of anti-Semitism are most apt to occur.

There is another area that could cause trouble between American Jews and the Gentile majority. From the inception of the state of Israel, both the United States government and the bulk of its citizenry have supported the Jewish homeland. For a number of reasons, the United States has backed the Israelis in their myriad of difficulties—militarily, as the Jewish state has battled for its right to exist in a hostile region; politically, in the United Nations; and economically, as Israel has struggled to remain viable. So long as the policies of the two nations remain tolerably in accord, each desiring the same ends secured through the same means, all is well. But what if the means and ends pursued by Israel become totally divorced from the national interests of the United States? A hint of this possibility emerged in the oil boycotts of the 1970s. Some bumper stickers of the era advised, "Put a Jew in Your Gas Tank." The Palestinian uprisings of 1988 have caused similar tensions.

More importantly, some Gentiles question the loyalty of American Jews, saying they would side with Israel against the United States. They unknowingly echo the philosophy of Adolf Hitler to this topic: Jews are never loyal to any nation, only to the idea of Zionism, or today, the nation of Israel. These people believe that in a period of crisis or peril Jews cannot be trusted. In view of the injustices that befell Japanese-Americans during World War II, it is possible for overt actions against Jews to occur if there were a U.S.-Israeli conflict of interests.

The problem is compounded by the nature of Judaism itself, which upholds Jewish nationhood as a basis for being, together with God and the Torah. This fact means that people such as some Arabs and Soviets who claim that they are not anti-Semitic but only anti-Zionistic are not being realistic. This use of semantics is a risky practice; above and beyond the play with words, it could form a means of isolating Jews as enemies because of their support for Jewish nationhood when this course is not popular with mainstream policy.[7]

What concrete, constructive, and effective steps can society take to ensure that the Holocaust will never be repeated? Beyond the continuing need for individuals and groups to combat anti-Semitism whenever and wherever it occurs, other measures are also needed. It is very important to show non-Jews that anti-Semitism is not just a "Jewish problem" but one that affects the United States as a whole and its allies in the free world. The nations that evidence the most animosity toward Jews and the Jewish state also tend to dislike the American government. Thus, it is important whenever possible to stress *the link between American best interests and those of Jews.*

Another means of helping to ensure that the Holocaust never recurs rests with education efforts. Surely a tragedy that involved the loss of millions of lives cannot be adequately covered in a paragraph or two in school texts. Rather, the Holocaust and the events that led to its inception deserve full-scale treatment. The way in which anti-Semitism, and indeed bias against any group, can produce wholesale slaughter is a lesson all schoolchildren should be exposed to in their formative years.

The perceptions of the older population should not be ignored either. Various measures can be taken to choke off those seeds of hatred that still exist between peoples. While television shows about the Holocaust and media coverage of the trials of Nazi war criminals still being tracked down aid in keeping the memory of mass genocide before the public, it is possible to use simpler but still effective measures. *Community exchanges,* such as exhibits of religious customs and practices, break down walls of isolation and differences. It is, after all, the alien and outsider image that hampers understanding and friendship among groups. We should encourage any vehicle of communication between Jews and Gentiles that acts as a door opener to overcome centuries of barriers.

Another step that would help to counter anti-Semitism is something Jews have historically done: *offering assistance to other minority groups*. At times, even the best of relationships tend to become thin and frayed—as with blacks at present—but nevertheless such links can function as buffers to prejudice. More is at stake than simply helping other underdogs. The entire system of ethics and values that has governed the Jewish people from time immemorial includes the credo of freedom and justice for all. The drive to divert any possibility of a future Holocaust is only as strong as the weakest link in a democratic structure; danger for one group represents a danger to all who are in the minority by virtue of race or religion.

Nor should blacks, the traditional recipients of Jewish friendship, aid, and understanding, be the sole allies in the future. Hispanics offer a new and fertile field in forging community bonds, as do recent Asian immigrants. The latter, who are oriented in much the same direction as Jews—with strong commitments to home, family, and education, and with large numbers who own or seek to own small businesses—offer Jews an ideal opportunity to act as role models in the process of Americanizing these virtues while gaining friends as well.

One of the most controversial steps that some Jewish people have taken to inhibit a new Holocaust is overt militancy, both in America and Israel. The Jewish Defense League, led by Rabbi Meir Kahane, who is also head of the extremist Kach movement in Israel, is the prime instance of radical response to anti-Semitism. In Kahane's view, the best means of preventing a new Holocaust in the form of the violent ending of the Jewish state is to dispossess all Arabs from Israel. But to many, this approach appears to make Israel an oppressor with respect to the Arab minority; in other words, Jews who adopt this method are seen as imitating the Nazis. It is likewise questionable as to whether aggressively countering each act of anti-Semitism in the United States will create more world respect for Jews.

NOTES

[1] Dennis Prager and Joseph Telushkin, *Why the Jews?: The Reason for Antisemitism* (New York: Simon & Schuster, 1983), pp. 189-90.

[2] Lucy Dawidowicz, *The War Against the Jews* (New York: Holt, Rinehart and Winston, 19 75), pp. 3-5.

[3] Nathan Glazer, "Social Characteristics of American Jews," *American Jewish Yearbook*, vol. 56 (1955), p. 9.

[4] Stephen Steinberg, *The Ethnic Myth: Race, Ethnicity, and Class in America* (New York: Atheneum, 1981), pp. 230-36.

[5] Steinberg, pp. 236-40.

[6] Roberta Strauss Feuerlicht, *The Fate of the Jews* (New York: New York Times Books, 1983), pp. 122-23.

[7] Stephen D. Isaacs, *Jews and American Politics* (Garden City, N.J.: Doubleday, 1974), pp. 69-75.

Chapter 10:
Jesus Was a Jew

"And Joseph also went up from Galilee, out of the city of Nazareth, into Judaea, unto the city of David, which is called Bethlehem; (because he was of the house and lineage of David)"
(Luke 2:4).

Many Christians have difficulty accepting Jesus as a Jew. It would seem difficult, however, for Christians to evade a clear and simple fact: Jesus was born a Jew, of Jewish parentage and descent, extending back to the royal house of King David. Moreover, Jesus remained a practicing Jew all his life, observing the religious customs and obeying the tenets of that faith in every particular. It was the Jewish prophets who, through their revelations, created the necessary foundation for the belief in Jesus as the long-expected Messiah, the longed-for deliverer of the Jewish people. And finally, the apostles, the first leaders of the Christian church, were all Jews.

The Jewish nation as a whole did not follow the Christian faith, and by the second century A.D. Gentiles predominated numerically in the church. Over time, Christendom as a whole deviated from its Jewish monotheistic roots, the doctrinal and ethical teachings of Jesus, and the experience of the apostles.

Because many Jews had rejected the Messiah and His message, later church fathers decided that Jews no longer had the right to be God's elect. They began to feel that since those Jews had refused to recognize Jesus, this somehow indicated that Jesus was no longer "one of them," but had become "one of us." Many churchmen began to portray Jesus as venting divine anger at all Jews for not heeding His words. In the Gospel of John Jesus charged that the hypocritical Pharisees were not of God but of the devil, and this statement was later misinterpreted as a condemnation of all Jewish people.[1]

Clearly, in the mind of some professing Christians, and increasingly with those of later eras, Jesus had chosen to distance Himself from His Jewish heritage. The effect of such misinterpretation was to confirm that Christ was not actually a Jew at all. Hence, there was no reason to have to accept Him as such.

The intimate relationship between religion and art provided another piece of machinery for sustaining the popular sentiment that Jesus was somehow not a Jew. Art served religion by creating visible symbols of man's faith in the invisible or in what he could not truly know. In harmony with Old Testament injunctions and like the Jews, the early Christians did not use religious images for fear of idolatry, but by the sixth century Pope Gregory the

Chapter 10 – Jesus Was a Jew

Great greatly modified this policy. The break between Catholic and Jew in this area occurred because, the Pope stated, most people were unable to read or write and had to rely on pictures and images to teach them the history and the substance of the faith. Most of the representations that emerged depicted Jesus, His family, and His followers in aspects that departed considerably from Jewish appearances. Blond hair, blue eyes, and Nordic features, so evident in Gothic paintings, removed Jesus from His background quite effectively.

When Christians examined these portrayals, they could feel quite comfortable with the idea that Jesus, as visible in that picture, could not be a Jew. He looked just like them.[2] There was no need, no compulsion to accept the unpalatable, nay, the repulsive truth—their Savior had been a Jew. This notion was strengthened by illiteracy, which made it impossible for the ordinary person to turn to the sources of the faith and discover the truth. And, up until quite recent days, few Christian clergy stressed the origin of Jesus to their flock.

Yet other reasons for denying the Jewishness of Christ can be noted as well. Anti-Semitism is, of course, interconnected with racism. Long before the rise of Nazi Germany, many people in the ancient world preached the inferiority of certain ethnic groups. The Jews, although the product of many races, were often labeled as one of the "lower derivation" orders of mankind. Even where there were no Jews, such prejudice and misconceptions were widespread. To believe that God had permitted Himself to be incarnated as a member of a despised and "depraved" people was clearly impossible. Since Christendom was able to separate Jesus from His race, no sin or shame need be attached to labeling Jews as a lower form of humanity. If Jesus had been identified as a member of this cursed group, persecution of the Jews as a racial category would have been much more difficult.[3]

The effect of the denial of the Jewishness of Jesus is plain: it permitted people to ignore basic tenets taught by Jesus Himself, namely, that all men are brothers, that all should be loved, respected, and treated with dignity—both Jew and Gentile. In practice, professing Christendom has usually reflected the realities and the actions of the secular community; it has followed, indeed frequently initiated, the oppression or even destruction on occasion of a race held to be outside the pale of common fellowship. Set apart from Christianity's Jewish roots, the concept of Jesus as non-Jew found, and still finds, easy acceptance in some quarters of the so-called Christian world.[4]

NOTES

[1]Rosemary Reuther, *Faith and Fratricide* (New York: Seabury Press, 1974), pp. 115-16.

[2]E.G. Holt, *A Documentary History of Art* (Garden City, N.Y.: Doubleday, 1958), pp. 55-67.

[3]Joshua Trachtenberg, *The Devil and the Jews* (New York: Meridian Paperback, 1961), pp. 144-49.

[4]Charles Y. Glock and Rodney Stark, *Christian Beliefs and Anti-Semitism* (New York: Harper & Row, 1966), pp. 37-41.

Chapter 11: Judaism Today

As Catholic theologian Hans Kueng has said, without Judaism there would be no Christianity. Jesus' gospel presupposes the Torah and the Prophets, and therefore there has always been a special relationship between Jews and Christians. There has been collaboration between the two communities, but the Jews lived in mortal fear all over Europe during the first two crusades and the pogroms in Palestine and Eastern Europe. A change in this oppressive situation for the Jews came about only after the French Revolution, and the first real emancipation for the Jews took place in America. It should be noted that anti-Judaism persisted in Rome and Moscow, for different reasons. Rome could not tolerate anti-Christians, and Moscow was godless in its adherence to communism.

With the spread of the Industrial Revolution, there was an increased awareness of the universal brotherhood of man, and communism taught that this brotherhood extended across state boundaries. However, in reality, communism turned out to be a new form of imperialism. The nineteenth century was a melting pot of humanitarianism as well as oppression, emancipation as well as bondage. The battle cries of Marx and Engels did little to help the Jews who were the target of oppression both in Moscow and Germany, in addition to Spain and Portugal. It was only somewhat later that a semblance of real humanitarianism developed, and that mostly on American soil.

In the medieval ghetto, a good Jew was one who conformed to the "mitzvah" (Jewish law) system in all aspects of life. Jewish law encompassed civil as well as criminal matters and a moral code of conduct. In other words, scriptural and rabbinic law dealt with all aspects of life. Jews at first were granted self-government but were later granted citizenship by the individual states where they resided and were thus brought under state law. But problems soon arose because no one, including the state, had the authority to alter Jewish law. In medieval situations, a good Jew was one who scrupulously and precisely observed all the rabbinic law to the last detail.

With changes in society, great pressure arose to modernize and adjust these detailed rules. Thus in the modern world, people professing the Jewish faith found themselves breaking Jewish laws, to the extent that they made a distinction between the ethical and ceremonial laws. Orthodox Judaism could hardly condone such a distinction, which was undoubtedly one of convenience.

However, there arose several gradations within traditionalism itself: thus there are today not only traditionalists (the Orthodox), but ultratraditionalists (fundamentalists, or Hasidists). There are also the Reform or Liberal Jews, who have abandoned many Jewish regulations regarded as ceremonial or outmoded, and the Conservatives, who are in between the two extremes. Even though significant distinctions exist among these different sects, they are not always rigidly maintained:

> In truth, these distinctions have become quite fluid; in the United States, often the difference is in the character of the synagogue worship, whether Orthodox Conservative, or Reform, and not in the quantity of quality of one's personal observance of the mitzvah system. By and large in the United States, Orthodox, Conservative and Reform Jews all live alike, few of them in strict fidelity to the mitzvah system.... Most Jews in our day, being an urban people, are as pious in a Jewish way as are the urban people of Christian origin in a Christian way. Synagogues are almost as empty as churches, and would be just as empty were all external pressures on Jews suddenly removed, and sociological peculiarities made to vanish.[1]

Orthodox Judaism, or the official Jewish establishment, held sway in Western and Central Europe, and to a lesser extent Eastern Europe, around the mid-eighteenth century under the leadership of such people as Samson Raphael Hirsch and, earlier, Jacob Frank. There was also Israel Baal Shem Tov who tried to raise religious expression toward a new pietistic height in Hasidism. There were the inevitable social distinctions even within Orthodoxy, whereby the learned and the unlearned and the rich and the poor stood in opposite camps. It took quite a while for the rifts, including immigration to the New World, to heal.

The *Haskala* or the Enlightenment movement within Judaism emphasized westernization and reform of religion. The Reform, or Liberal, movement may be said to have started during the Napoleonic period, around the first decade of the nineteenth century. Reform came because of the incompatibility of Orthodox Jewish rituals with westernization. The old forms of worship were no longer acceptable to young Jews in Germany and the U.S. In Germany, the movement was institutionalized and gradually diminished. In the U.S., however, by 1880 almost two hundred synagogues came under its influence. Soon afterward came the Pittsburgh Platform and a manifesto to chart a new course for followers. In 1937, came the Columbus Platform with a similar message. By the 1950s, however, the Haskala more or less became a spent force with respect to further modification.

Conservative Judaism, unlike Enlightenment rationalism, was born of romanticism. It began in 1845 when Zacharias Frankel and his followers seceded from a second Reform synod at Frankfurt. They wanted to retain the historic use of Hebrew for prayers. The Conservatives agreed with Reform Jews that Judaism was a developmental religion, but they held that it was nevertheless closely attached to traditional observances.

In studying Jewish thought today and the relationship between Judaism and Christianity, it is important to understand the Messianic tradition in Judaism. In ancient

Judaism, there were explicit and implicit teachings about the coming of the Messiah to redeem the Jewish people. God promised to deliver the land of Israel to the people and said that He was the one God of all mankind. In order to fulfill this "eternal covenant," the Scriptures promised that the Messiah would come. Thus Messianic redemption became one of the major affirmations of biblical religion. When the Messiah apparently did not come in accordance with Jewish expectations, the rabbis tried to reconcile the traditional Messianic element with some difficulty. They said that the Messiah did not come because "man was in no fit spiritual state to experience it." But this argument implied that the Messiah would arrive at a later date for sure. There was no doubting the Word of God and its proclamation of a Messianic age to come:

> The meaning and content of the Messianic age are summed up for the whole of Jewry in the fact that world-history will move on into a period in which evil will be annihilated and God's will shall be fully acknowledged throughout the world. This comprises three things: first, that within the people of God a process of separation will begin, the ungodly will disappear and perish.... Secondly, the Messianic age would mean that the dispersion of Israel amongst the Gentiles would come to an end... and, finally, that the people of the Law would no longer be enslaved by the nations who despise God's will, but they would pay homage to Israel and its God.[2]

Messianism reflects the most powerful motivations of Jewish life because of its psychological roots in the Jewish people. Two opposing motivations seem to coexist in messianism, one affirming the return of Israel to its status in the days of David and Solomon and the other utopian or apocalyptic. The Messianic ideal is present in Genesis 1:31: "And God saw every thing that he had made, and, behold, it was very good." According to the first view, if this world is not perfect, at least it can be perfected, because it is man's role to become "a partner of the Lord in the work of creation." The reason for the existence of evil is to test man in his attempts to overcome it and facilitate God's design. The second, utopian view, however, is the opposite of this: this world is wicked, and God must intervene to redeem it and the faithful.

Throughout the medieval and early modern periods, messianism remained a "blend of hope and despair." People like Maimonides insisted that the Messianic age would come about in the normal course of events, while Nahmides claimed that there would be a resurrection to mark the beginning of the Messianic era. Hasidism was both supernatural and Messianic but was at the same time progressive in its outlook. Mystical unifications could expedite the arrival of the Messiah. The Orthodox today also believe in the coming of the Messiah, even though the state of Israel pursues secular policies in general. But the state of Israel itself could be a sign of the Messianic age.

Authorities claim that the Messianic movement is gathering strength in the U.S., and it interprets events and phenomena like the unenviable plight of the P.L.O., Zionism, and the U.N. as preparation for the arrival of the Messiah. The impact of the Holocaust was somewhat reduced by notions of liberalism deeply engraved in the American Jewish psyche. They now enjoy the good life based on liberalism and human rights. However, they "cannot but feel the unbearable tension between the two basic world-views," both rooted in their heritage.

Messianism is an old phenomenon in Judaism. The Orthodox, Reform, and Conservative movements all had their origins in the hope that the disasters they suffered were only transient and that a glorious, promised future lay in store for the people of Israel. In fact, it is this hope that seems attractive to the young American Jew today, not the piety or the ritual or the prayer as such.

After years of oppression and anti-Semitism and statelessness in Europe, Jews today are thankful for what is available to them in the New World. They have contributed significantly to the prosperity of the land in a very diligent manner in arts, science, and philosophy.

The three major centers of Jewish culture in the world today are Israel, the Soviet Union, and the United States. Judaism is one of the three major American faiths along with Roman Catholicism and Protestantism. However, in the United States traditional Judaism is being progressively secularized, thanks to the open society and the "melting pot" ideology. To retain their original identity, Jews constantly draw upon the state of Israel for religious fervor and inspiration.

Many young Jews today are taken up with the symbolic significance of messianism. It is an enabling rather than disabling faith. Jewish teachers proclaim that there should be an "individualized enactment of the mores of the Messianic age" before it is actually ushered in, which could in itself expedite the arrival of the Messiah. The philosopher Maimonides suggested that the idea of a Messianic era could be "a spur to human resourcefulness to tap all of our strategies by way of historically actualizing mankind's most cherished dreams of peace and self-mastery. "

Messianism has an inherent attraction for the modern Jew in terms of what it offers now as well as what it promises for all time. In his prayers, for example, he is aware of the importance of redemption and immortality "as central categories of Jewish faith." And that faith, especially since the time of Maimonides, is enshrined largely in the Messianic concept. The *Hakol Yodukha* prayer, which is recited every Shabbat, originally expressed this hope of redemption clearly:

> There is none to be compared unto Thee, neither is there any beside Thee; there is none but Thee: Who is like unto Thee? There is none to be compared unto Thee, O Lord our God, in this world, neither is there any beside Thee, O our King, for the days of the Messiah; neither is there any like unto Thee, O our Savior, for the resurrection of the dead.

Previously, the laws of repentance stated, "The ultimate and perfect reward, the final bliss which will suffer neither interruption nor diminution is the life of the world to come" (*Hilkhot Teshuvah*, 9:2). But Maimonides adds to this a clear statement as to the certainty of the Messianic era: the Messianic era, by contrast, will be realized in this world, which will continue its normal course except that independent sovereignty will be restored to Israel. The ancient sages had already said, " The only differences between the present and the Messianic era is that political oppression will cease." Thus the interpretation of Maimonides has contributed in a large measure to the present popularity of Messianic Judaism in the United States.

Messianic Judaism is a natural result of biblical prophecy. For example, Daniel 9:25 states, " Know therefore and understand, that from the going forth of the commandment to restore and build Jerusalem unto the Messiah the Prince shall be seven weeks, and threescore and two weeks: the street shall be built again, and the wall, even in troublous times."

Many other Old Testament writings make reference to the Messiah, and the New Testament presents Jesus as the fulfillment of those prophecies. The ritual blood sacrifice of the Old Testament as described in Leviticus 17:6—"And the priest shall sprinkle the blood upon the altar of the LORD at the door of the tabernacle of the congregation, and burn the fat for a sweet savour unto the LORD"—are replaced in Christianity by the shedding of the blood of Jesus. Jesus said to His disciples at the Last Supper, "This is my blood of the new testament, which is shed for many" (Mark 14: 24), "This cup is the new testament in my blood, which is shed for you" (Luke 22:20). The New Testament states that redemption comes through the shedding of Christ' s innocent blood to atone for the sins of humanity. "For God so loved the world, that he gave his only begotten Son, that whosoever believeth in him should not perish, but have everlasting life" (John 3: 16).

New Testament Christianity proclaims that salvation comes when a person applies Christ's redemptive work to his own life by accepting Jesus as Lord, believing upon Him, and obeying His gospel.

Christ exhorted, "I am Alpha and Omega, the beginning and the ending.... Behold, I stand at the door, and knock: if any man hear my voice, and open the door, I will come in to him, and will sup with him, and he with me. To him that overcometh will I grant to sit with me in my throne, even as I also overcame, and am set down with my Father in his throne. He that hath an ear, let him hear what the Spirit saith unto the churches" (Revelation 1:8; 3:20).

The Apostle Peter told an assembly of Jews how they could accept Jesus as Lord and Christ and receive salvation from sin through Him: "Repent, and be baptized every one of you in the name of Jesus Christ for the remission of sins, and ye shall receive the gift of the Holy Ghost" (Acts 2:38).

Spirit-filled believers in Jesus, both Gentile and Jewish, are laying a common-ground foundation that eliminates the disease of anti-Semitism. It is a foundation rooted in the love of the Messiah Jesus, the love from God that flows through His Spirit-filled believers.

NOTES

[1] Hans Kueng, *Christians and Jews* (New York: Seabury Press, 1974), pp. 48-49. Much of the preceding discussion is also based on this source.

[2] Werner Foerster, *From Exile to Christ* (Philadelphia: Fortress Press, 1964), p. 193. Subsequent quotations are also from this source.

Chapter 12: Monotheistic Christianity as Judaism's Heir

"Hear, O Israel: the LORD our God is one LORD"
(Deuteronomy 6:4).

The concept of the oneness of God permeates both Old Testament and New Testament thought. The concept of a trinity, or three persons in the Godhead, was not part of the thinking of the Jews, apostles, or the early church. It was first officially adopted into Christendom at the Council of Nicea in A.D. 325 in reaction to the Arian heresy that Jesus was a created being capable of both good and evil. The Nicene Creed as modified by the Council of Constantinople in 381 is now the official orthodoxy of Roman Catholicism, Eastern Orthodoxy, and the Church of England, as well as many other Protestant churches.[1]

A careful examination of the Scriptures, however, does not support the Trinitarian dogma. Practically speaking, an individual may have multiple functions or relationships such as that of a father, brother, and son, and yet he remains one person. Similarly, God has three roles, functions, or relationships to mankind—Father, Son, and Holy Spirit—but yet He remains one and the same being. In addition to Deuteronomy 6:4, many verses of Scripture emphasize this truth: "See now that I, even I, am he, and there is no god with me" (Deuteronomy 32:39). "O LORD of hosts, God of Israel, that dwellest between the cherubims, thou art the God, even thou alone, of all the kingdoms of the earth: thou hast made heaven and earth" (Isaiah 37:16). "God is one" (Galatians 3:20). "For there is one God, and one mediator between God and men, the man Christ Jesus" (I Timothy 2:5). "There is one lawgiver, who is able to save and to destroy" (James 4:12). (See also Isaiah 42:8; 43:10-11; 44:6-8, 24; 45:6, 18, 21-22; 46:9.)

These statements refer to the one true God of Israel (and of the world). Of course, He has many names, such as Adonai, Elohim, El Shaddai, and Yahweh. The greatest of His names is Jesus, or Yeshua in Hebrew, which means Yahweh-Savior, for Jesus was actually the one God incarnate.

The concept of Jesus as the one God, the Father, manifested in flesh is substantiated in both the Old Testament and the New Testament.[2] "For unto us a child is born, unto us a son is given: and the government shall be upon his shoulder: and his name shall be called Wonderful, Counsellor, The mighty God, The everlasting Father,

The Prince of Peace" (Isaiah 9:6). "He that hath seen me hath seen the Father" (John 14:9). "I and my Father are one" (John 10: 30). (See also Isaiah 7:14; 63:16; Micah 5:2; John 1:1, 14; 20:28; Acts 9:5; Titus 2:13.)

The doctrine of the trinity was not the only errant concept to creep into Christendom. Another concept that is still prevalent today is the belief that when a Jewish person becomes a follower of Yeshua, he or she is no longer a Jew but forfeits any claim to Jewish identity. On the contrary, not only was Yeshua a Jew, so were all of His original followers. The whole movement for the first several years of its existence was a movement within Judaism.[3] In fact, except for Luke, all the writers of the New Testament were Jews.

The Book of Acts describes the Jewish followers of Yeshua in these terms: "Thou seest, brother, how many thousands of Jews there are which believe; and they are all zealous of the law" (Acts 21:20). We know from other accounts of history that Jewish followers of Yeshua after biblical times remained Hebraic, law-keeping communities, in most cases.[4] Jewish heritage and identity were compatible with following Yeshua.

Yeshua never rejected His Jewish heritage, nor did He ever deny the validity of the Torah. To the contrary He said, "Think not that I am come to destroy the law, or the prophets: I am not come to destroy, but to fulfil. For verily I say unto you, Till heaven and earth pass, one jot or one tittle shall in no wise pass from the law, till all be fulfilled. Whosoever therefore shall break one of these least commandments, and shall teach men so, he shall be called the least in the kingdom of heaven: but whosoever shall do and teach them, the same shall be called great in the kingdom of heaven" (Matthew 5:17-19).

At this point some may wonder why God decided to have a chosen people. He wanted a people who would be obedient to Him and who would, through their prophets and leaders, prepare the way for the Messiah. He wanted a people set apart from the rest of the world with the determination to be faithful to their covenant with Him. To initiate this special plan, God chose the great man of faith, Abraham. He told him, " Get thee out of thy country, and from thy kindred, and from thy father's house, unto a land that I will shew thee: and I will make of thee a great nation, and I will bless thee, and make thy name great; and thou shalt be a blessing: and I will bless them that bless thee, and curse him that curseth thee: and in thee shall all families of the earth be blessed" (Genesis 12:1-3).

Through Yeshua, the descendant of Abraham, the blessing of salvation is indeed offered to all the world, not only to the Jews, but also to the Gentiles. Simon Peter, one of the leading disciples, had a divine vision that convinced him that God's love and salvation were to be offered to the Gentiles without them having to become Jews in the sense of abiding by all of the ceremonial regulations of the Torah (Acts 10-11). Rabbi Saul (Paul), a student of Rabbi Gamaliel I, had a miraculous encounter with the Lord and was commissioned to bring the message of Yeshua to the Gentiles (Acts 9:15).

The conversion of many Gentiles prompted a council of leaders to discuss Gentile participation in the movement. After much deliberation, they accepted the

Gentiles without requiring them to adhere to standard Jewish practices such as circumcision (Acts 15).

Over the centuries, the Christian church as a whole departed from the original faith and experience, and the result was a stale church with many erroneous and pagan elements. As a political institution it not only distorted and destroyed the Jewish elements of the early church, but it later participated directly or indirectly at various times in the attempted destruction of the Jewish people as well.

The Apostle Paul, in one of his letters to the early church at Rome, described what it meant to be a true Jew in the early church: "For he is not a Jew, which is one outwardly; neither is that circumcision, which is outward in the flesh. But he is a Jew, which is one inwardly; and circumcision is that of the heart, in the spirit, and not in the letter; whose praise is not of men, but of God" (Romans 2:28-29). A person whose heart is filled with the Spirit of the Messiah is circumcised in the heart and becomes a descendant of Abraham by faith, regardless of his or her natural heredity (Romans 4:9-17). The Gentile believers were grafted into the original olive tree that grew from the roots of the Hebrew patriarchs. "Thou, being a wild olive tree, wert grafted in among them, and with them partakest of the root and fatness of the olive tree" (Romans 11:17).

Speaking of unbelieving Israel, Paul wrote, "And they also, if they abide not still in unbelief, shall be grafted in: for God is able to graft them in again" (Romans 11:23). In fact, Paul referred to Isaiah 59:20 to assure his readers that a time would come when Israel as a nation would receive Yeshua as their Messiah and be delivered:

"And so all Israel shall be saved: as it is written, There shall come out of Sion the Deliverer, and shall turn away ungodliness from Jacob: For this is my covenant unto them, when I shall take away their sins" (Romans 11:26-27).

Paul summarized his discussion of God's plan of salvation for both Jews and Gentiles by saying, "For God hath concluded them all in unbelief, that he might have mercy upon all. O the depth of the riches both of the wisdom and knowledge of God! how unsearchable are his judgments and his ways past finding out!" (Romans 11:32-33). With our finite minds we cannot understand the mind of God, but according to His Word Israel will be saved, at least those Jews who accept Messiah Yeshua and obey Him.

When Yeshua returns to earth as promised, all the Jews will have a chance to see and choose the Messiah. "Behold, he cometh with clouds; and every eye shall see him, and they also which pierced him: and all kindreds of the earth shall wail because of him" (Revelation 1: 7). Surely at that time few of the seed of Abraham, when brought face to face with Messiah Yeshua, will deny Him. Paul indicates that it will be a great day of salvation for Jews and also a tremendous blessing to the Gentiles who believe (Romans 11:15).

Paul himself had a face-to-face, miraculous encounter with God on the road to Damascus that changed him from a persecutor to an apostle. This overwhelming experience with the Spirit of God is still able to transform the hearts and minds of people today. The next chapter will explain how I discovered this truth and received this experience in my own life.

NOTES

[1] Bruce Shelly, *Church History in Plain Language* (Waco, Texas: Word Books, 1982), p. 116.
[2] David Bernard, *The Oneness of God* (Hazelwood, MO: Word Aflame Press, 1983), p. 66.
[3] Hugh Schonfield, *The History of Jewish Christianity* (New York, 1933), Chapter 3.
[4] Irenaeus, *Against the Heresies* (a second-century work).

Chapter 13:
The New Anti-Semitism

Through the pages of history over the last two thousand years, anti-Semitism has left its bloody stains. From the inquisitions in Spain to the pogroms of Russia, it climaxed in Nazi Germany and the horrific destruction of six million Jewish lives in the Holocaust. Foundational in the culture of anti-Semitism, within the European church and with the so-called reformers, such as Martin Luther, was the fallacious doctrine of "replacement theology."

This doctrine taught that the Old Testament prophecies regarding the Jewish people and Israel were conditional and were transferred to the church (i.e. the church replaced Israel as recipient) because of Israel's rejection of the Messiah. Building a narrative of hate against the Jews was simplified if it could be shown that even their Creator had rejected them. However, key Old Testament prophecies related to Israel are accompanied by the Hebrew word *olam*, which means everlasting and not conditional. (See

#5769 in Strong's Concordance.) Consider the following verses of Scripture:

> And I will establish my covenant between me and thee and thy seed after thee in their generations for an everlasting [*olam*] covenant, to be a God unto thee, and to thy seed after thee. And I will give unto thee, and to thy seed after thee, the land wherein thou art a stranger, all the land of Canaan, for an everlasting [*olam*] possession; and I will be their God (Genesis 17:7-8).

Furthermore, it is noteworthy that scholars who study biblical prophecy have discovered and proved what they term a "Prophetic Law of Multiple Fulfillment," in which a prophecy can have *more than one* fulfillment. For instance, a prophecy can have a primary audience and fulfillment, and yet also have a secondary audience and fulfillment, and perhaps even a tertiary, and so forth. Bible readers who don't know about the fact of multiple fulfillments can get confused when they see biblical prophecies related to Israel (for instance, pertaining to a future time period of the Jews, namely during the prophesied worldwide Millennial Kingdom age) having a secondary fulfillment for the church *prior* to the primary fulfillment for the Jews. Just because a prophecy to the Jewish people has not been fulfilled yet, and a secondary fulfillment has already occurred, does not mean the church has replaced natural Israel and does not mean the prophecy will not eventually have its primary fulfillment pertaining to Israel.

Chapter 13 – The New Anti-Semitism

For several years after the Holocaust and the demonic destruction of six million men, women, and children, there seemed to be an abatement of virulent anti-Semitism. Scenes of the death camps and testimonies of Holocaust survivors brought much sympathy and compassion for the Jewish people. However, in 1948, Israel's Declaration of Independence brought an immediate attack from Israel's surrounding Islamic neighbors.

Against all odds Israel miraculously survived and eventually became a strong democracy in the Middle East. It grew financially, militarily, and governmentally through its democratic institutions and its rule of law. Israel continues to be surrounded, bullied, and attacked by its Islamic neighbors and has been portrayed through fallacious propaganda as the aggressor, the perpetrator against the Palestinians, and ultimately the source of all problematic issues in the Middle East.

This fallacious pro-Palestinian narrative has become a centerpiece and source of propaganda in the new anti-Semitism. The people promoting this propaganda deny that they are anti-Semitic. They say that they are just anti-Zionist, resisting the sovereignty and legitimacy of the state of Israel. This new anti-Zionist (anti-Israel) narrative deceitfully repackages the age-old venom and hatred for the Jews as a righteous movement against what they call an apartheid state of Zionist Israel.

The connection between this anti-Zionism and anti-Semitism is described in a Wikipedia entry about the phrase *new antisemitism*, which states in part: "the concept [is] that a new form of antisemitism has developed in the late 20th and early 21st centuries, emanating simultaneously from the far-left, radical Islam, and the far-right, and tending to manifest itself as opposition to Zionism and the State of Israel."[1]

Scholars at the Hoover Institution of Stanford University have studied and commented extensively on this new anti-Zionist, anti-Semitic phenomenon. An example is an article by Victor Davis Hanson, who is the Martin and Illie Anderson Senior Fellow in Residence in Classics and Military History at the Hoover Institution and also a syndicated columnist for the Tribune Media Service. Mr. Hanson wrote an article titled "The New Anti-Semitism," subtitled "Why does the international community hate Israel so much?"

In the article he reflects that, "The new anti-Semites are not crass and vulgar. They are sophisticated intellectuals.... no longer just buffoonish skinheads, neo-Nazis, and Klansmen, but... polished and sophisticated intellectuals.... [They speak] not of disliking Jews, but only of despising the Jewish state."[2] Within this new anti-Semitism one can see a paradigm shift: hatred that previously was directed toward Jews individually now is focused on the nation of Israel and coupled with a motivation that seeks the destruction of Israel.

The attack methods of these anti-Zionists include propaganda warfare with a simple rehashing of the old "replacement theology" in which Israel is replaced by the church. This doctrine is being used by the ultra liberal Christian churches and others in the development of a one-sided, pro-Palestinian, anti-Zionist narrative.

To achieve their desired results (such as Israel's giving up of land) these anti-Zionists have developed several punitive measures against Israel. These include boycotts of Israeli products, divestments of companies doing business with Israel, and economic sanctions against Israel.

In addition, they are attempting to stop any government—especially the United States—from helping Israel financially or militarily. Those who support these punitive measures say that they are not anti-Semitic; they claim they are simply opposing Zionism and the sovereignty of an apartheid Jewish state.

However, if their plan of boycotts, divestments, and sanctions weakens Israel financially and militarily to the point that the Israelis are unable to defend themselves against hostile surrounding neighbors, the result will be another holocaust. Their so-called "BDS" tactics (boycotts/divestments/sanctions) are either extremely naive in thinking they will bring peace or very heinous in their real assessment of the potential destructive results.

The Anti Defamation League (ADL), an American Jewish organization, has identified an anti-Zionist organization called the Sabeel Group as number three on a list of the top ten anti-Israel, anti-Semitic groups operating in America and elsewhere. The ADL cites a Sabeel-hosted conference in 2004 titled "Challenging Christian Zionism: Theology, Politics, and the Palestinian Israel Conflict."[3] The ADL indicates that the Sabeel organization has provided the structure to bring together extreme liberal American and European clergy, along with both radicalized Palestinian Christians and Muslim groups, in order to attack Israel.

It was indicated that Sabeel's 2004 conference had more than 600 participants from 32 countries. The thesis of the conference was, "Christian Zionism Justifying Apartheid in the Name of God." According to a conference spokesman, "God's special connection with the Jews became irrelevant following the appearance of Jesus." (Such is but a repackaging of replacement theology.)

The Sabeel spokesman explained that the separation happened "as a judgment for their [Jews'] failure to recognize Him [Jesus] as the Messiah," in addition to their "otherwise sinful ways." Furthermore, the spokesman advanced the notion that the contemporary Jews living in Israel are just as sinful and rebellious as their fore-fathers and thus "deserve the same fate" (i.e. either destruction or exile).

In conclusion, the Sabeel spokesman stated, "The present brutal, repressive, and racist policies of the state of Israel would suggest another exile on the horizon rather than a restoration. How sinful do you need to be to be on God's hit list?"

Even within the Evangelical church, there is growing evidence of the proliferation of this new anti-Zionist, anti-Semitic phenomenon. Dr. Paul Wilkinson, in his book, *The Church at Christ's Checkpoint*, responded to the worldwide anti-Zionist conference held in Bethlehem, March 9-12, 2012 titled, "Christ at the Checkpoint."[4]

Dr. Wilkinson wrote much about the prime movers and shakers at this conference, noting that the common thread throughout their discourse is the disclaimer that they are not anti-Semitic but in fact, anti-Zionist—simply resisting Israel as an illegal apartheid state. However, when one watches videos that have come out of this conference, in listening to the key speakers one senses a feeling of disrespect and animosity that they seem to have for the Jewish people and their traditions.

While viewing one of the videos of this conference, two respected rabbis from the Simon Wisenthal Jewish Center were motivated to write an article that was published in "The Times Of Israel, Daily Edition" newsletter. Rabbis Abraham Cooper and Yitchok Adlerstein titled their article, "Jeers and Loathing in Bethlehem: a presentation by a respected Evangelical author last month shows that some Palestinian boosters are willing to take us back to the darkest days of adversus Judaeous."[5] The rabbis see the arrogant mocking of Jewish people and their traditions as innately anti-Semitic.

It would be wise for all who call themselves Christians to heed the words of the great rabbi, the Apostle Paul, who spoke to Christians on behalf of the Jewish people:

> For if the firstfruit is holy, the lump is also holy; and if the root is holy, so are the branches. And if some of the branches were broken off, and you, being a wild olive tree, were grafted in among them, and with them became a partaker of the root and fatness of the olive tree, do not boast against the branches. But if you do boast, remember that you do not support the root, but the root supports you. You will say then, "Branches were broken off that I might be grafted in." Well said. Because of unbelief they were broken off, and you stand by faith. Do not be haughty, but fear. For if God did not spare the natural branches, He may not spare you either. There-

fore, consider the goodness and severity of God: on those who fell, severity; but toward you, goodness, if you continue in His goodness, otherwise you also will be cut off (Romans 11:16-22).

The Bible is clear about those who arrogantly mock and boast against the Jewish people and Israel that they will be cut off spiritually! Conversely the Bible is also clear about those who bless Israel and the Jewish people. Speaking of Abraham and the Jewish people the scripture says:

> And I will make of thee a great nation, and I will bless thee, and make they name great; and thou shalt be a blessing: And I will bless them that bless thee, and curse him that curseth thee: and in thee shall all families of the earth be blessed (Genesis 12:2-3).

It is clear from the word of God that as we bless Israel and the Jewish people, we will also be blessed!

NOTES

[1] Wikipedia Internet Encyclopedia, "New Anti-Semitism" http://en.wikipedia.org/wiki/New_antisemitism (current as of September 13, 2013)

[2] Hanson, Victor Davis, "The New Anti-Semitism" (The Hoover Institution, Stanford University, March 28, 2012)

[3] Anti Defamation League website, "Sabeel Ecumenical Liberation Theology Center" (and ADL Backgrounder, 2008)

[4] Wilkinson, Paul, *The Church at Christ's Checkpoint* (Cheshire, UK: Hazel Grove Full Gospel Church, April, 2012)

[5] Cooper, Abraham and Yitchok Adlerstein, "Jeers and Loathing in Bethlehem" (The Times of Israel, April 5, 2012)

Chapter 14: My Experience

My experience with Yeshua was, like Paul's, miraculous in nature. I had believed intellectually in a prophet Jesus, the Son of the Trinity, a concept that I could not completely comprehend nor could those who attempted to teach it to me. To them it was also a mystery, a "holy mystery." In this confused state in which I had accepted Jesus, some told me that I had attained a conversion experience wherein I would be saved.

I also attended a religious college with very high standards. However, we were taught that the experiences, lives, and acts of the apostles in the New Testament were of a different dispensation, or age, from ours. There was never any discussion of the Jewishness of Jesus, of the apostles, or even of the Early Church. I was taught that the gifts of the Spirit that they experienced were not available today: miracles of healing and speaking in tongues were not for us. I accepted what I was taught, but thought that this teaching seemed to contradict the Bible. For example, after describing the gift of the Holy Spirit that he had just received with the sign of speaking miraculously in a language he had never learned, the Apostle Peter declared, "For the promise is unto you, and to your children, and to all that are afar off, even as many as the Lord our God shall call" (Acts 2:39).

It was evident that there was a clear distinction between what my teachers taught and what the Bible said. Doubt permeated my thinking, for I knew that I did not have the power to live a holy life for God. When a friend asked me to join him in his work in an inner city ministry, I had to decline his offer—not because I didn't want to help, or because I didn't feel that God was calling me, but because I knew that I did not have the spiritual power necessary for that work, and I did not want to be a hypocrite.

In the following twenty years I went into business and learned the trade of tent-making from my father. In addition to weekly church attendance, I contributed time and money beyond the norm, but Yeshua was not the Lord of my life. Eventually sin in various forms became so overpowering in my life and in the lives of my loved ones that I reached a point where I felt I could no longer carry on in life. I had the material things that money could buy, but that was not enough. We seemed to be sinking in quicksand.

At that time, while traveling on the road and feeling completely distraught, I pulled over to a rest area and began to pray in a way that I had never prayed before, crying out to God. My prayer was simple: "Jesus, I believe you

Chapter 14 – My Experience

are real. Please take over my life. If you will heal my family and help me straighten out my affairs, I will serve you." Within weeks many miraculous things began to happen to my family, to me, and to my business. These extraordinary blessings came as an answer to prayer and substantiated in my life the reality of Jesus as the Messiah.

This was not the end of the story, but just the beginning. I had promised to serve Jesus, and I intended to do just that, but I had to be remolded and chastened. "For whom the Lord loveth he chasteneth, and scourgeth every son whom he receiveth. If ye endure chastening, God dealeth with you as with sons" (Hebrews 12:6-7).

At this time a young man invited me to a United Pentecostal Church. He stated that he had been a cocaine addict and that Jesus had miraculously healed him at one of the church services. He also said that his story was not exceptional, that among the approximately one hundred members of his local church, there were many such testimonies among the men and women. They included former alcoholics, cocaine addicts, and a mainline heroin addict who had all been completely delivered and were now living new lives in Jesus. I was impressed, but I did not go to the church immediately.

Two months passed, and as time went on I kept thinking about my commitment. I finally went to church, and at first it was a shocking experience. The people seemed to me to be extremely emotional: shouting praises to Jesus, crying, and clapping hands to the solid beat of a hymn called "There is Power in the Blood." If that were not enough, the preacher began to preach at what seemed like a deafening intensity. But then his message shifted to the Jews, God's chosen, His jewels. He talked with a love toward them that demonstrated a special kinship between Pentecostals and Jews. He further described a special love for Israel in general and the city of Jerusalem in particular. I was deeply touched, for I had never heard anyone in any Christian church talk about love for the Jewish people, and I had visited churches of most of the major denominations at one time or another. To hear a preacher talk about Jerusalem as the spiritual home of Christians was amazing to me.

My family and I were deeply moved by God in that service, as evidenced by our tears. After that day, however, we began to hear about the church's desire for holiness and certain standards of conduct, which now seem simple but then seemed insurmountable. Of course, without the indwelling Holy Spirit, any real, permanent standard of holiness is impossible to maintain. The Holy Spirit will lead a person to the right choices, and the standard then comes from within.

I did not understand the principles of the Spirit-filled life at that time, however, so we tried a Trinitarian Pentecostal church, but the services there seemed dead in comparison. Afterward, my six-year-old daughter cried and said, "Daddy, can we go back to the little church where Jesus was?" When my wife and I heard that we laughed, but we knew what it meant. The next week we were back at Faith United Pentecostal Church. I began to enjoy the loud praising. In fact, I remembered reading that King David shouted praises to God, and wasn't he a man after God's own heart? (I Samuel 13:14).

Chapter 14 – My Experience

Months passed, and although I repented to some degree, I did not receive the Holy Spirit. I believed that I knew the reason. I could not set aside my attachment or love of worldly things. It took six months for me to make a total commitment and repent fully. On the night that I was baptized in Jesus' name, having His name called over me, I had what many call a charismatic experience. I was filled with the Spirit of God and spoke in tongues just as the Early Church did in Acts 2:4. Thus I obeyed and experienced the New Testament plan of salvation that the apostles preached. (See Acts 2:38.)

A sense of peace and joy ensued. I knew now that I had the power to live for God. I had His Spirit in me. I could understand now the meaning of the verse of Scripture that says, "Be not drunk with wine, wherein is excess; but be filled with the Spirit" (Ephesians 5:18). The peace and joy I felt was better than any artificial high I had previously experienced. It was a secure feeling to know that I had been reconciled to God, eternally saved through the sacrifice that Yeshua made on Calvary's cross, through the shedding of His precious blood. The feeling is best described as "joy unspeakable."

This joyful salvation is available to all who hunger for it and are willing to humble themselves. Scripture states that this promise of salvation, strange as it may seem to some, is to the Jew first and then to the Gentile. "For I am not ashamed of the gospel of Christ: for it is the power of God unto salvation to every one that believeth; to the Jew first, and also to the Greek" (Romans 1:16).

It is my prayer that this book will help some to come as I did into the presence of the Almighty Yeshua, be forever transformed by His touch, and experience the salvation that He provides. When they do, they will truly live as chosen people of the one true God and become the spiritual heirs of Abraham.

Dedication & Thanks

Dedication and kudos first and foremost to Esther, my wife of 48 years, who fits the biblical model in Proverbs 31 of the virtuous and righteous woman. Her spiritual support and editorial help made this book a reality.

Kudos to Bishop David M. Hudson for getting us and a host of other ministers to Israel and motivating us to stand for and support Israel and the Jewish people.

Kudos to Rev. Donald D. Hanscom for his passion and work in multicultural ministries, including Jewish.

Kudos to Rev. David J. Sagil for his leadership and infectious enthusiasm for Jewish relations.

Kudos to my former pastor, Rev. John W. Davis, who encouraged me to write about my Jewish roots.

Finally, kudos to Dr. David K. Bernard for his steady hand as one of the foremost leaders in the body of Christ today.

Bibliography

Adler, H.G. *The Jews in Germany*. Notre Dame, Ind.: Notre Dame University Press, 1969.

Anti Defamation League. "Sabeel Ecumenical Liberation Theology Center": ADL website and ADL Backgrounder, 2008.

Baron, Salo W. "Medieval Folklore and Jewish Fate," *Jewish Heritage Reader*, Edited by Lily Edelman. New York: Taplinger Publishing Co., 1965.

Bendersky, Joseph W. *A History of Nazi Germany*. Chicago: Nelson-Hall Publishing Co., 1985.

Bernard, David K. *The Oneness of God*. Hazelwood, Mo.: Word Aflame Press, 1983.

Bickerman, Elias J. "The Historical Foundations of Post-Biblical Judaism," *The Jews: Their History*. 4th ed. Edited by Louis Finkelstein. New York: Schocken Books, 1977.

Broszat, Martin. "National Socialism, its Social Basis and Psychological Impact," *Upheaval and Continuity*. Edited by E. J. Peuchtwanger. Pittsburgh: University of Pittsburgh Press, 1974.

Coates, James. *Chicago Tribune*, September 8, 1985.

Cooper, Abraham and Yitchok Adlerstein. "Jeers and Loathing in Bethlehem." The Times of Israel, April 5, 2012.

Dawidowicz, Lucy. *The War Against the Jews: 1933-1945*. New York: Holt, Rinehart, and Winston, 1975.

Dimont, Max. *The Jews in America*. New York: Simon and Schuster, 1978.

Eban, Abba. *The Story of the Jews*. New York: Behrman House, 1968.

Feingold, Henry. *The Politics of Rescue*. New Brunswick, N.J.: Rutgers University Press, 1970.

Feuerlicht, Roberta Strauss. *The Fate of the Jews*. New York: New York Times Books, 1983.

Flannery, Edward H. *The Anguish of the Jews*. New York: Macmillan, 1965.

Glazer, Nathan. "Social Characteristics of American Jews," *American Jewish Yearbook*, Vol. 56 (1955).

Glock, Charles Y., and Rodney Stark. *Christian Beliefs and Anti-Semitism*. New York: Harper and Row, 1966.

Gordon, Milton M. *Assimilation in American Life*. New York: Oxford University Press, 1964.

Gordon, Sarah. *Hitler, Germans and the "Jewish Question."* Princeton, N.J.: Princeton University Press, 1984.

Grayzel, Solomon. *A History of the Jews*. New York: Mentor Books, 1968.

Hanson, Victor Davis. "The New Anti-Semitism." Stanford University, The Hoover Institution, March 28, 2012.

Heider, F. *The Psychology of Interpersonal Relationships*. New York: Wiley, 1963.

Hilberg, Raul. *The Destruction of European Jews*. New York: Quadrangle Press, 1961.

Holt, E. G. *A Documentary History of Art*. Garden City, N.J.: Doubleday, 1958.

Isaacs, Stephen D. *Jews and American Politics*. Garden City, N.J.: Doubleday, 1974.

Irenaeus, *Against the Heresies* (a second-century work).

Katz, Jacob. *Exclusiveness and Tolerance: Jewish-Gentile Relations in Medieval and Modem Times*. New York: Shocken, 1962.

Levine, Naomi and Martin Hochbaum. *Poor Jews*. New Brunswick, N.J.: Transaction Books, 1974.

Mahl, G. F. *Psychological Conflict and Defense*. New York: Harcourt, Brace, Jovanovich, 1971.

Prager, Dennis and Joseph Telushkin. *Why the Jews?: The Reason for Antisemitism*. New York: Simon and Schuster, 1983.

Reuther, Rosemary. *Faith and Fratricide*. New York: Seabury Press, 1974.

Roth, Cecil. *A History of the Jewish People*. Oxford: East and West Publications, 1935.

Sachar, Abram. *A History of the Jews*. New York: Knopf, 1974.

Schoeps, Hans J. *The Jewish-Christian Argument*. New York: Holt, Rinehart and Winston, 1963.

Schonfield, Hugh. *The History of Jewish Christianity*. New York, 1933.

Schweitzer, Frederick. *A History of the Jews*. New York: Macmillan, 1971.

Shelly, Bruce. *Church History in Plain Language*. Waco, Texas.: Word Books, 1982.

Shibutani, Tomatsu. *Society and Personality*. Englewood Cliffs, N.J.: Prentice-Hall, 1968.

Shirer, William L. *The Rise and Fall of the Third Reich*. New York: Simon and Schuster, 1960.

Silberman, Charles. *A Certain People*. New York: Summit, 1985.

Sklare, Marshall. *America's Jews*. New York: Random House, 1971.

Sontheimer, Kurt. "The Weimar Republic—Failure and Prospects of German Democracy," *Upheaval and Continuity*. Edited by E. J. Feuchtwanger. Pittsburgh: University of Pittsburgh Press, 1974.

Sowell, Thomas. *The Economics and Politics of Race*. New York: Quill, 1983.

Steinberg, Stephen. *The Ethnic Myth: Race, Ethnicity, and Class in America*. New York: Atheneum, 1981.

Tarachow, Sidney. "A Note on Anti-Semitism," *Psychiatry*. Vol. 9 (1946).

Taylor, Simon. *The Rise of Hitler*. New York: Universe Books, 1983.

Trachtenberg, Joshua. *The Devil and the Jews*. New York: Meridian Paperback, 1961.

Volkman, Ernest. *A Legacy of Hate: Anti-Semitism in America*. New York: Franklin Watts, 1982.

Weisel, Elie. *A Jew Today*. New York: Random House, 1978.

Wikipedia Internet Encyclopedia. "New Anti-Semitism." http://en.wikipedia.org/wiki/New_antisemitism Current as of September 13, 2013.

Wilkinson, Paul. *The Church at Christ's Checkpoint.* Cheshire, UK: Hazel Grove Full Gospel Church, April, 2012.

Made in the USA
Lexington, KY
23 June 2017